THE KOREAN WAR

W9-AJM-444

Twentieth-Century Wars
General Editor: Jeremy Black

Published
Peter Lowe   *The Korean War*

Forthcoming
D. George Boyce   *The Falklands War*
Gerard DeGroot   *The First World War*
William Maley   *The Afghanistan War*
Ritchie Ovendale   *The Gulf War*

Twentieth-Century Wars
Series Standing Order ISBN 0–333–77101–X

You can receive future titles in this series as they are published by placing a standing order. Please contact your bookseller or, in case of difficulty, write to us at the address below with your name and address, the title of the series and the ISBN quoted above.

Customer Services Department, Macmillan Distribution Ltd
Houndmills, Basingstoke, Hampshire RG21 6XS, England

THE KOREAN WAR

Peter Lowe

© Peter Lowe 2000

All rights reserved. No reproduction, copy or transmission of
this publication may be made without written permission.

No paragraph of this publication may be reproduced, copied or
transmitted save with written permission or in accordance with
the provisions of the Copyright, Designs and Patents Act 1988,
or under the terms of any licence permitting limited copying
issued by the Copyright Licensing Agency, 90 Tottenham Court
Road, London W1P 0LP.

Any person who does any unauthorised act in relation to this
publication may be liable to criminal prosecution and civil
claims for damages.

First published 2000 by
MACMILLAN PRESS LTD
Houndmills, Basingstoke, Hampshire RG21 6XS
and London
Companies and representatives
throughout the world

ISBN 0-312-23304-3   paperback

A catalogue record for this book is available
from the British Library.

This book is printed on paper suitable for recycling and
made from fully managed and sustained forest sources.

10	9	8	7	6	5	4	3	2	1
09	08	07	06	05	04	03	02	01	00

Printed in Hong Kong

Typeset in Great Britain by Aarontype Limited, Easton, Bristol

Trasnferred to Digital Printing 2007

Contents

List of Maps

Preface and
Acknowledgements

This volume aims to provide a concise survey of the origins, nature and aftermath of the Korean war. The most controversial issues concern the origins and the first twelve months of the war. How did the conflict occur? What were the assumptions and priorities of those men holding influential positions in each of the states principally involved? Why did the conflict develop from the existing civil war into an international struggle involving the United Nations? How is the peculiar character of the war to be explained with such rapid reversals of fortunes for both sides in the course of its first twelve months? Why did the struggle in the Korean peninsula not escalate into a larger conflict, as the hatred and suspicion of the Cold War intensified? How was an armistice agreement reached in 1953 but why was no political settlement possible?

These are some of the crucial questions addressed in this volume. The approaching fiftieth anniversary of the outbreak of the war will focus debate on these issues in the context of a war which has not preoccupied historians, political commentators or the media to the extent of the Vietnam war. However, the Korean conflict took place at one of the most dangerous periods since the end of the Second World War and, had political leaders not demonstrated some degree of caution, following the errors and miscalculations accompanying the origins of the war, it could have expanded into a third world war.

While I was involved in the later stages of writing this volume, I was fortunate enough to meet some of the American and British veterans who had fought under the flag of the United Nations in Korea. In February 1999 I participated in a one-day school organised by the Department of Continuing Education in the University of Oxford and met a number of British veterans. It was most helpful to exchange views with them and to hear how deeply they had been affected by their experiences between 1950 and 1953. I was also happy to meet Rosemary Foot and Geoffrey Warner once more and I benefited from hearing their presentations. In March 1999 I attended a conference reassessing the Korean war, at Cantigny, Wheaton, Illinois, one of a series organised jointly by the Robert R. McCormick Tribune Foundation and the US Naval Institute. It was a great pleasure to participate in this event and to meet American veterans, retired or serving officials and fellow historians. It was illuminating to be able to compare the recollections of former American officers with those of the British veterans I had met a short time before. This was furthered by the presence at Cantigny of General Sir Anthony Farrar-Hockley, a distinguished veteran and the official British military historian of the war. Among other fellow historians I benefited from hearing the opinions of Chen Jian, Bruce Cumings, Roger Dingman, Richard Hallion, Arnold Offner, William Stueck and Kathryn Weathersby. It was equally valuable to meet Ambassador Donald Gregg, John Merrill and Don Oberdorfer. I wish to thank Carol Mason for all the hard work she put into the organisation of the conference and to thank all the staff at Cantigny for their enthusiastic assistance.

I am most grateful to the editor of this series, Professor Jeremy Black, for his keen perusal of the text and suggested improvements which I have sought to incorporate. I am also grateful to Terka Bagley, the history editor at the publishers, for her efficiency and encouragement. Keith Povey has provided invaluable assistance once more, as editorial services consultant.

Finally, it is again a pleasure to thank Jean Davenport for her efficiency and zeal in typing the manuscript.

Manchester   PETER LOWE

Every effort has been made to trace the copyright holders but if any have been inadvertently overlooked the publishers will be pleased to make the necessary arrangement at the first opportunity.

List of Abbreviations

CCP	Chinese Communist Party
CIA	Central Intelligence Agency (United States)
DPRK	Democratic People's Republic of Korea (North Korea)
KMAG	Korean Military Advisory Group
NATO	North Atlantic Treaty Organisation
NKPA	North Korean People's Army
NKWP	North Korean Workers Party
NNRC	Neutral Nations Repatriation Commission
NNSC	Neutral Nations Supervisory Commission
NSC	National Security Council
POWs	Prisoners of war
PRC	People's Republic of China
ROK	Republic of Korea (South Korea)
SCAP	Supreme Commander for the Allied Powers, Japan
SKWP	South Korean Workers Party
UN	United Nations
UNC	United Nations Command
UNCOK	United Nations Commission on Korea
UNCURK	United Nations Commission for the Unification and Rehabilitation of Korea
UNTCOK	United Nations Temporary Commission on Korea

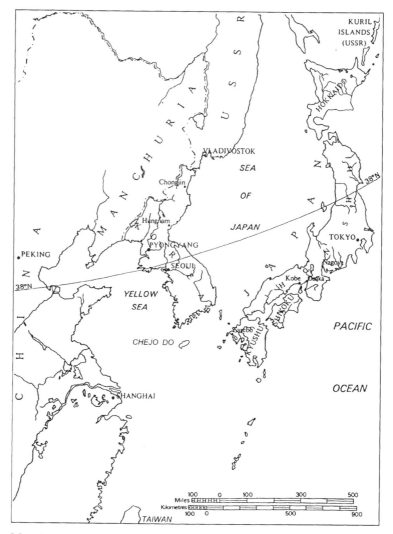

Map 1 *Korea and eastern Asia*

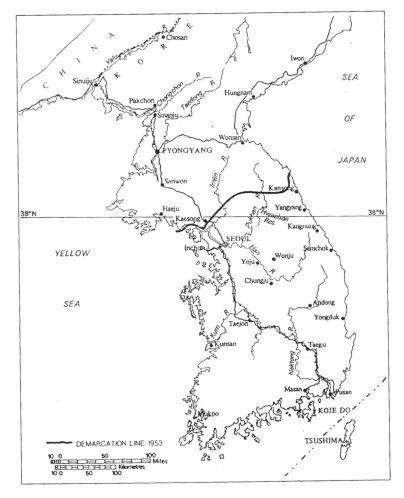

Map 2   *Korea, 1950–53*

Introduction

The Korean war lasted a little over three years, from June 1950 to July 1953. It was the most significant conflict to occur during the Cold War and it helped to determine the course of the Cold War. The Korean struggle was simultaneously a civil war and an international war: Syngman Rhee and Kim Il Sung represented the passionate desire of left and right to see their country reunited, after the arbitrary decision to divide Korea at the 38th parallel, implemented in August–September 1945. At the same time the great powers pursued their rivalries in the context of Korea, as in other parts of the globe. The Soviet Union encouraged the Democratic People's Republic of Korea (DPRK) to attack the Republic of Korea (ROK) in June 1950 and the United States decided not only to intervene but to ensure that the United Nations [UN] acted. The aim of this volume is to explore how the Korean war occurred; to examine the principal characteristics and nature of the war; and to consider the consequences of the war. This introduction discusses briefly certain of the most interesting issues and personalities with the intention of setting the scene for the more detailed consideration to follow.

For the DPRK (North Korea) the war connoted a bold, if reckless, attempt to secure unification swiftly through force of arms. If the advance had succeeded, Korea would have been unified with a combination of communism and nationalism prevailing, as interpreted by Kim Il Sung. For the ROK (South Korea) the war comprised a dire threat to its existence, followed by the enticing prospect of securing unification through the liquidation of the DPRK, as UN (mostly American) forces moved north, in conjunction with the ROK army, towards the Yalu river. Both Korean states experienced analogous feelings of exhilaration and despair in the first four months of war. Thereafter, each was compelled to appreciate that unification was impossible to achieve and that a

1

compromise settlement would be unavoidable. For the Soviet Union the war constituted the failure of one of Stalin's few great gambles in the international sphere; however, the war also underlined the role of fundamental importance played by Russia in coordinating the reactions of communist states and in helping to determine that the DPRK would survive. American and British leaders acknowledged on key occasions that the war could only be brought to an end through enlisting the cooperation of the Soviet Union. For the United States the war represented a qualified achievement in preventing the forcible elimination of a state pledged to resist communism: the achievement was qualified because the endeavour of the UN (controlled effectively by the United States at this time) to inflict decisive defeat on the DPRK and the People's Republic of China (PRC) failed, to the chagrin of the Americans.

For the UN the war demonstrated that the young organisation was capable of acting with greater resolution than its ill-fated predecessor, the League of Nations, but only because of the ineptitude shown by the Soviet Union at the start of the war in not moving to block the American decision to mobilise the UN. However, the reality was that the UN was dominated by the United States, and the sixteen states contributing forces under the UN flag were compelled to recognise that the best they could hope to achieve was to exert marginal influence on the direction of American policy. As an organisation, the UN was weakened rather than strengthened through its role in Korea before and during the war. For China the war connoted a calculated gamble which largely, but not entirely, succeeded. China demonstrated unequivocally that it was a major force to be reckoned with and that it could not be marginalised by its principal opponent or its principal ally: the United States and the Soviet Union came to accept that China was now a prominent actor on the Asian stage.

The Korean war is intriguing for reminding us once more of the impact of personality upon historical processes. Syngman Rhee and Kim Il Sung were deeply committed nationalists, each inspired (as was Mao Tse-tung in China) by the bitterness and passion engendered by foreign subjugation: lasting hatred of Japan, as the recent colonial master of Korea, was accompanied by resentment that each Korean state had to rely on the aid of outside powers, yet the humiliation was softened by the belief that the powers could be manipulated to help in securing the wider objectives of the ROK and the DPRK. Both Rhee and Kim revealed much guile and tenacity in exploiting the major powers. Rhee obtained massive American military assistance between 1950 and 1953, followed by a permanent military alliance and large-scale economic aid. Kim obtained substantial Russian help, including covert Soviet air intervention and the involvement of vast Chinese armies. After 1953 Kim proved more successful than Rhee and Rhee's successors in escaping from foreign influence, as he skilfully played the Soviet Union and China off against one another. On the other hand, the ROK gained more in the long term through strengthening its economy as a result of cooperation with the United States. Stalin took the most fateful decision of any individual leader when he decided to encourage Kim Il Sung in the latter's endeavour to fulfil his ardent ambition to unite Korea. Stalin thus set in motion a chain of events that led inexorably to the localised eruption of the Cold War into a hot war. The failure of his gamble meant that Stalin drew back from subsequent direct action in Korea: his later initiatives were designed to protect the DPRK without involving the Soviet Union in developments that could mark escalation into a third world war. Stalin urged Mao to commit Chinese forces on a large scale to Korea but the Soviet role was confined mostly to the air where it was easier to conceal the extent of the Soviet contribution.

Harry Truman (President of the United States, April 1945–January 1953) was a staunch opponent of communism and a political leader of courage and obstinacy. He did not exercise the degree of control over policy evinced by Stalin: Dean Acheson, the American secretary of state, was responsible for defining the chief characteristics of American foreign policy at the end of the 1940s and it was Acheson who handled the immediate reactions in Washington, DC, following the outbreak of the war. But Truman both approved the actions decided by Acheson and personally took the vital decisions committing American forces to action in the Korean peninsula on his return from Independence, Missouri, to Washington. During the later tergiversations, as the military pendulum swung back and forth, Truman stood firm on the vital features as he discerned them – there would be no evacuation of the peninsula and there would be no betrayal (as he saw it) of prisoners of war (POWs) who had no wish to return to the states for which they had fought. Truman's decision on the latter issue contributed significantly to the prolongation of the war and to the extent of the defeat suffered by the Democratic party in the presidential election of 1952. The American commitment to mobilise resources fully for a possible third world war later in the 1950s gained momentum powerfully under the Truman administration. General Eisenhower, who was elected to the presidency in November 1952, viewed matters in a broadly similar way to Truman: they had worked quite closely together until Eisenhower decided to support the Republican party. However, Eisenhower was adamant that the Korean war must be terminated instead of dragging on interminably. A widespread weariness among most of the participants was probably more important than Eisenhower's impatience in achieving the signing of an armistice in July 1953 (even then Syngman Rhee remained strongly opposed to an armistice and refused to sign it).

Mao Tse-tung took the most important decision after those taken by Stalin, Kim Il Sung and Truman in 1950. Mao concluded in October 1950 that the PRC must intervene militarily in the Korean struggle in order to assert China's rediscovered pride and confidence after a century of humiliation and subjugation to foreign powers. Vital Chinese interests were at stake in Manchuria, in addition to which Mao was deeply affronted by American intervention to prevent the PRC from assuming control of the island of Taiwan, the last stronghold of Kuomintang (Chinese Nationalist) forces led by Chiang Kai-shek. Mao was under no illusions concerning the magnitude of the decision he was taking. A number of his senior colleagues argued that it was not wise for the recently established PRC to fight the strongest power in the world, but Mao saw the war in Korea as an opportunity to demonstrate to the United States, the UN and the Soviet Union that China was an important player in Asian affairs in a far more meaningful sense than had been the case a decade earlier when Chiang Kai-shek postured as a leader in exchanges with Franklin Roosevelt and Winston Churchill. Mao succeeded in establishing China's importance but at a cost greater than he envisaged in October 1950.

Clement Attlee and Winston Churchill were minor figures in the context of the Korean war in comparison to the leaders considered above. Great Britain was the next most important participant in UN military operations after the United States but the scale of British military commitment came a long way behind the American contribution. Attlee's principal impact lay in his dramatic visit to Washington to meet President Truman in December 1950, at a time when it was feared that the United States might deploy nuclear weapons in Korea. Attlee conveyed the depth of concern in Britain and in western Europe as well as in the Commonwealth and emphasised the necessity for consultation between allies. This occurred during a traumatic phase of much uncertainty regarding the future direction of American policy. Churchill's contribution was heroic and original, yet this related to more general anxiety over the Cold War rather than Korea itself. After the death of Stalin, in March 1953, Churchill was enthused with the newly opening opportunity to diminish the dangers of the Cold War leading to another world war and he acted with tenacity to foster exchanges with the new Soviet leaders. Part of this process involved securing an armistice in Korea. At a time when Syngman Rhee was causing much embarrassment in seeking to block conclusion of an armistice agreement, Churchill communicated with Moscow and stressed that Rhee's shrill protests must be disregarded in pursuance of the more profound issues involved. Churchill's zeal for *détente* annoyed Eisenhower but arguably was important for convincing the Soviet Union that the UN wanted the Korean war brought to a conclusion.

Events in Korea revealed the extent of miscalculation and error by each state involved in the more fundamental decisions that led to the conflict and its escalation. But it also showed a maturity of judgement in appreciating the dangers of allowing matters to go too far. The Korean conflict was the most dangerous war to occur since 1945 and, with the exception of the Cuban missile crisis in 1962, contained the most perilous occasions for propelling the world into a global conflagration. This is why, as we approach the fiftieth anniversary of the outbreak of the war, it is worth examining again the nature and course of the savage struggles that so divided and devastated this remote peninsula in East Asia between 1950 and 1953.

1

The Gathering Storm

For much of the twentieth century Korea has been the victim of racial discrimination. Between 1910 and 1945 Korea was part of the Japanese colonial empire. Japan itself was a victim of racial pressure and was subjected to western imperialism in the second half of the nineteenth century and in some respects down to the start of the Great War in 1914. The West continued to regard Japan as inferior until the events of 1941–2 transformed attitudes dramatically. Japan itself acted with racial superiority towards the regions it annexed and occupied between 1895 and 1943. During the Korean war UN forces, particularly American troops, referred condescendingly to the 'gooks', thus continuing the racial stereotypes of the Pacific war and anticipating those to be seen in the Vietnam war. The common image of Korea was that of a downtrodden, poverty-stricken peninsula, divided by two hostile regimes, motivated respectively by support for communism or antagonism to it. Korea was regarded with a mixture of sympathy and contempt. This was transformed by the resilience and determination shown by both Korean states after 1953. The ROK was transformed into a formidable economic power within a generation. The DPRK advanced economically at first but later fell back during the 1980s: it was and remains a powerful militaristic state resting on a fervent ideology comprising nationalism, communism and indigenous culture plus the eccentric continuation of Kim Il Sung's ideology.

The success of the two Korean states after 1953 underlined the faith in Korea's future and a fierce zeal to reassert Korean independence. Prior to the bitterness and savagery of the twentieth century, Korea had been unified for over a thousand years. A potent sense of cultural cohesion existed notwithstanding strong regional distinctions. The monarchy presided over the destiny of the people and one dynasty prevailed from 1392 until Japanese annexation in 1910. The Yi dynasty was originally vibrant but declined progressively from the seventeenth century. It survived in part because of its client relationship with China and because of an absence of strong challenge internally. Confucianism was the most important influence upon the evolution of Korean society. A sense of hierarchy and status was created and sanctioned: the contribution of the *yangbon* (aristocracy) was legitimated. Gregory Henderson, an American diplomat and historian, produced one of the most fascinating surveys of Korean culture and society, enlivened by the comparison drawn between past and more recent patterns of behaviour [45]. Bruce Cumings has written the most satisfactory one-volume history of Korea, enriched by his deep knowledge of the country [18]. Henderson and Cumings emphasise the enduring effects of the *yangbon*. Confucianism created a hierarchy and a doctrine of reciprocal obligation. In practice, Confucianism was a conservative ideology yet possessing sufficient flexibility to function successfully over a very lengthy period. This relationship worked in the interests of each state until it collapsed amidst the more marked decline of the Ch'ing and Yi dynasties in the second half of the nineteenth century. The peasants were, as always, exploited in the interests of the monarchy and *yangbon*. As in China, peasant grievances accumulated and manifested in growing rebellion. Korea resembled China and Japan in experiencing accelerating decline internally just as the western powers began their powerful thrust into eastern Asia.

The Japanese impact

However, what was interesting and ominous about Korea's situation was the aggressive approach revealed by Japan soon after the Meiji restoration of 1868. Japan was subjected to western imperialism, but a number of Japanese leaders wished to develop Japanese imperialism, with Korea as the first victim. The extent of divisions within ruling circles, plus the urgency of ending feudalism in Japan and fostering modernisation, diminished Japanese threats temporarily. However, Korea was forced to sign a treaty with Japan in 1876. This was the prelude to the more sinister Japanese involvement in Korea that developed in the 1880s and culminated in the annexation of Korea in 1910. Britain and the United States wished to secure the opening up of Korea and treaties were signed by Korea with both countries. During the 1880s Korea became the focal point for a grave collision of interests between China, seeking to maintain its traditional authority over Korea, and Japan, seeking to establish a sphere of its own. This led to the Sino-Japanese war of 1894–5 in which China was heavily defeated. Japan annexed the island of Taiwan and sought to consolidate its position in the Kwantung peninsula of Manchuria. Japanese ambition was frustrated via the triple intervention of Russia, France and Germany: Japan was compelled to relinquish certain of the gains conceded by China. Sino-Japanese rivalry was succeeded swiftly by Russo-Japanese animosity, leading to the Russo-Japanese war of 1904–5. The Japanese navy proved triumphant over its rickety Tsarist opponent and the Japanese army performed well in the savage fighting in Manchuria. The Russo-Japanese war ended, through the mediation of President Theodore Roosevelt, with a peace treaty signed at Portsmouth, New Hampshire. Japan established effective dominance of Korea in 1905 and this was followed by full annexation five years later. The worst fears of Korean patriots were realised as their country forfeited independence and became a colonial possession of Japan. Syngman Rhee, who had been a youthful conspirator against the Yi dynasty to which he was distantly related, began his lengthy and courageous condemnation of Japanese annexation.

Japanese rule had a positive side in addition to the obvious negative features. Japan provided an efficient administration in place of the inept Yi structure. A powerful stimulus was given to the future growth in the economy through the creation of effective communications and investment to promote the economy [18, pp. 162–74]. Industry was based mainly in the north while the south was predominantly agricultural. Education was developed with the aim of encouraging loyalty to the Japanese emperor in the spirit of state Shinto. At first the Korean language and literature was discouraged, but a more liberal approach developed in the 1920s and 1930s with the result that renewed patriotism bubbled beneath the façade of subservience to the Japanese authorities. This helps in explaining the ferment unleashed in Korea following the defeat of Japan in 1945 [16]. As was inevitable, numerous Koreans collaborated with the occupiers to protect or advance their own interests. Many landowners acquiesced in the Japanese presence; Korean conservatives often collaborated and this accounts for the prominence evinced by the Korean left in 1945. Syngman Rhee was one of the few who did not collaborate; instead he fulminated against the evils of Japanese rule from his various places of exile, latterly in the United States. Some ambitious Koreans joined the army and advanced their careers. Many of the officers in the ROK army, fostered by the United States after 1945, had served in the Imperial Japanese Army. Koreans served in the police force and acted as prison guards: certain of the latter were noted for their sadistic behaviour when they worked in POW camps during the Pacific war. The Korean police were widely hated and brutal retribution was meted out by the peasants in 1945 and after [16, pp. 166, 176–81, 298].

In all it may be said that Japan quickened greatly the pace of change in Korea and modernised its society. Japan also stimulated by reaction a burning patriotic zeal and concomitant determination to expel hated colonialism and to rebuild a new unified and independent Korea. This aspiration could only be attained through the defeat of Japan in the Pacific war. It was clear from 1943 onwards that Japan was losing the war, but it was wholly unclear as to how long this process would take. The European war was the priority for the United States and Britain, and Japanese troops continued to fight with their customary dedication and commitment [96]. The allies pledged themselves at the Cairo conference in 1943 to strip Japan of its colonial possessions, but the fate of Korea remained to be decided. President Franklin D. Roosevelt favoured the concept of trusteeship for former colonial territories and he seems to have placed Korea in the same category as Indo-China. Roosevelt's successor, Harry Truman, had no particular preferences and understandably took time to adjust to the demands of office, following the sudden death of his predecessor in April 1945 [98]. A decision of profound significance was reached in Washington in August 1945 when two American army colonels, one of whom was Dean Rusk, determined that the United States and the Soviet Union should occupy Korea, the division occurring at the 38th parallel [60, p. 19]. The Soviet Union had advanced against Japan one week earlier, following the dropping of the first atomic bomb on Hiroshima and just before the detonation of a second atomic bomb over Nagasaki. As matters turned out, the Soviet Union played a minor role in ending the Pacific war and certainly much less than envisaged by Roosevelt at the Yalta conference in February 1945. For Korea, however, the Soviet intervention was crucial in deciding its future. The decision to divide Korea at the 38th parallel was reached suddenly and was not intended to be permanent. In fact, subject to the limited border changes recognised when the armistice was signed in 1953, the division was permanent.

American and Soviet policies

The common feature in the response of the Korean people in 1945 was to wish their country united and independent. Zeal for basic change and reform was revealed in the formation of 'people's committees', a spontaneous upsurge of grassroots democracy. One person who promptly joined such a committee was Kim Dae-jung, perennial campaigner, ultimately elected president of the ROK at the end of 1997 [18, p. 361]. Because so many right-wingers had collaborated, the running was made by the left, fuelled by the determination to apply sweeping changes in Korean society. Had the foreign powers not intervened, it is probable that Korea would have developed into a radical state in 1945–6 and one which would have gravitated towards communism, since the right wing had little to offer. Part of this prediction was realised rapidly because of the Soviet occupation of North Korea, which rendered it straight-forward for communism to establish itself north of the 38th parallel (this begs the question of which *variety* of Korean communism would evolve, to which we shall revert shortly). American occupation of South Korea meant that any possibility of radicalism, let alone communism, succeeding south of the 38th parallel in 1945–6 was doomed. The American occupation forces arrived on 8 September 1945, three weeks after Emperor Hirohito announced the Japanese surrender. The Soviet army could have occupied South Korea and, indeed, did advance beyond the 38th parallel initially, but Stalin adhered to the division proposed by the United States. The American occupation was headed by General John Reed Hodge: he remained in command until shortly before the occupation ended [60, pp. 23–40]. Hodge hailed from rural Illinois and served with distinction during the Pacific campaigns. He was competent, reliable and loyal to General Douglas MacArthur, the Supreme Commander Allied Powers (SCAP) in Japan: the latter was perhaps the more important reason for his appointment [63; 49; 81]. MacArthur was engrossed in Japan and wanted a safe pair of hands (as he would define this concept) in control of Seoul. Hodge's virtues were that he was hard-working, direct in his approach, relatively uncomplicated, and genuine in his endeavours. His draw-backs were complete ignorance of Korea before arriving and a vehement hostility to communism, which made him unwilling to cooperate with the Soviet Union in fulfilment of the original aim of trusteeship. Hodge conceived of his mission as intended to bolster the Korean right, to give the latter time to adjust and find a credible leader or leaders and, above all, to prevent communism from coming to power south of the 38th parallel. In reaching this deci-sion on arrival, Hodge was in advance of the State Department which was committed to securing agreement with the Soviet Union. Trusteeship was unpopular in South Korea and Hodge was hostile to it in principle. He wanted urgently to find a rightist of credibility who would restore the cause of conservatism. There were two possibilities, Kim Ku and Syngman Rhee. Both were long-time campaigners who refused to collaborate with the Japanese. Rhee was the more devious and subtle of the two and gradually Rhee established his role. In so doing he became involved in growing differences of opinion with Hodge: Rhee had to show that he was not an American puppet and standing up to Hodge was one way of demonstrating his independence. Rhee required American support but this should be on his terms.

American–Soviet exchanges occurred from late in 1945 and led to the creation, in March 1946, of the Joint Commission as a means of securing agreement. The lengthy deliberations of the Joint Commission failed owing to mutual suspicion and growing acri-mony. Each side suspected the other of harbouring ulterior designs. The Joint Commission was soon revealed to be a futile body. American policy came to place more emphasis on Korea early in 1947 as the Cold War started to gain momentum. A committee comprising State and Treasury Department officials was created and a significant programme of aid was contemplated, broadly similar to that applied for Greece and Turkey [60, pp. 36–7]. It is relevant to note the contribution made by Dean Acheson, under–secretary of state, in 1947 [1]. Acheson displayed considerable interest in Korea and informed the Senate Foreign Relations Committee in March 1947 that a rolling programme of aid was required for Korea. American and British officials were alarmed at the deteriorating situation in Korea: the British were not consulted with any frequency by the Americans and officials in the Foreign Office doubted whether the Truman administration was committed sufficiently to defending Korea in the longer term [60]. Rhee consolidated his position as principal spokesman for the right and positioned himself skilfully for becoming the first leader of the South Korean state. Renewed attempts to obtain agreement between the United States and the Soviet Union were made when the Joint Commission met in May 1947. The exchanges failed since mutual suspicion had expanded; the aim of trying to map a way forward, on the lines approved originally at the Moscow conference in December 1945, ended with final recognition of the futility of pursuing this course.

Opinion in Washington inclined towards a combination of requesting the UN to observe developments in Korea and of reducing the American military commitment. The worsening of the situation in Europe as relations between the Soviet Union and the West steadily deteriorated [47] and an inability to define American objectives precisely enough combined to produce a muddled, ambivalent approach to Korea. On the one hand, Korea was important because it was one of two countries in the world where American and Soviet forces confronted one another directly, the other being Germany [86]. Dean Acheson did not want Korea to go communist. On the other hand, the pressure on limited American resources meant that the Pentagon was very reluctant to accept commitments in areas deemed non-essential. Air power should be capable of responding to a sudden crisis. This afforded another example of the consistent exaggeration of air power and what it could accomplish in terms of deterrence in this period. Furthermore, although the United States supported Rhee, doubts grew as to his judgement and reliability. Rhee enjoyed influential support in some American quarters. One of his close confidants was M. Preston Goodfellow, a leading figure in American intelligence during the Second World War and who was intimately involved in Korean affairs after 1945, as Goodfellow's private correspondence shows [59, pp. 168, 171, 182, 184; 18, pp. 194–6]. Certain American business circles supported Rhee and he was highly regarded in the right wing of the Republican party. The State Department and more liberal circles were less enthusiastic. Rhee's passion for Korean unification was such that it was feared that he might start a war in Korea if the opportunity arose, which in turn could drag the United States into conflict in Asia when Europe was regarded as the priority.

American attention focused, in 1947–8, on the role of the UN and preparations for the establishment of an independent state in South Korea. The UN was a fairly small body at this time and it was controlled by the United States. The formal aim was to achieve the creation of a unified state in which North Korea would consent to elections being held under UN supervision. A temporary UN commission (UNTCOK) was established in November 1947 despite Soviet opposition: the members comprised India, Canada, Australia, France, China, El Salvador, the Philippines and Syria with an Indian, Kumara P. S. Menon, as chairman. In December 1948 UNTCOK was replaced by a more permanent body (UNCOK), possessing the same membership except for Canada. The terms of reference for UNTCOK were to observe the process of conducting elections and to make recommendations regarding the creation of a unified Korean state. UNTCOK was faced with an impossible task. The Soviet Union and the communist administration in North Korea, led by Kim Il Sung, was opposed to the creation of UNTCOK. The United States and American officials in south Korea regarded UNTCOK as an American-inspired body which should act always in accordance with American wishes. Members of UNTCOK did not view their role in this light and friction sometimes occurred between the members and American representatives. The outcome of the elections held in South Korea in May 1948 was victory for the rightists. The elections were held in a raucous atmosphere amidst allegations of corruption and intimidation. UNTCOK did not possess enough personnel to observe the elections fully; the results were deemed valid for areas visited by members of UNTCOK but the resultant assembly was not recognised as a *national* assembly [62, pp. 235–6]. The ROK emerged in July 1948 with a constitution claiming to represent the whole of Korea. Rhee was elected as the first president. The UN General Assembly carried a resolution in October 1948 recognising the ROK. It was recommended that foreign troops should leave Korea and that negotiations should take place between both Korean administrations to secure a unified state. The ROK faced major political and economic problems. There was no stability in the new political structures and Rhee faced opposition on the right from the Korean Democratic Party [KDP]. Unrest existed in various parts of Korea and there was a danger of armed rebellion of the kind desired and encouraged by Kim Il Sung. The newly created army required much assistance in training and in provision of arms and equipment by the United States. The American military mission in Korea (KMAG) was a substantial body, the second largest American mission in the world, and was headed by

Brigadier-General Roberts. Roberts believed that the ROK army had become a reasonably efficient force by the summer of 1950, but his confidence was not borne out by experience following the start of the war. Inflation became a serious difficulty in 1949–50 and was ominously reminiscent of the problems that undermined the Kuomintang regime in China in the later 1940s. Rhee, however, implemented land reform in the spring of 1950, which was more than the Kuomintang achieved before 1949. One of the motives was to undermine the KDP, which was largely supported by landowners.

The situation along the 38th parallel was tense with periodic incidents for which both sides were responsible. The ROK army was described, in the period from 1948 to 1950, as weak, vulnerable and leaning heavily on the United States. The Truman administration would not give a binding undertaking to defend the ROK in the event of serious conflict erupting, because it feared that Rhee might regard such an agreement as facilitating a South Korean attack northwards with the purpose of achieving unification. Western observers were not sanguine on the future of the ROK. Officials in the British Foreign Office believed that, within a decade or so, the whole of Korea would be communist-controlled. MacArthur also spoke in similar vein on one occasion. It is hardly surprising that communist leaders regarded the situation in Korea as encouraging and that in 1950 they seized the perceived opportunity to implement their strategy.

At this point it is appropriate to discuss the progress of communism in Korea. Communist factions emerged soon after the Bolshevik revolution in Russia. They were characterised by acrid division and hatred [93]. Rival factions cooperated with the Soviet Union or with the Chinese Communist Party [CCP]: others pursued covert activities in Korea, in defiance of the Japanese police, or conducted guerrilla activities against the Japanese from bases in Soviet or Chinese territory which could overlap with the earlier-mentioned factions. While guerrillas caused embarrassment to the Japanese army, they represented no real threat to Japanese rule. The significance of the guerrillas is that they underlined the close association between communism and nationalism. The man who emerged as the key revolutionary leader was Kim Il Sung [92]. He was responsible for welding the disparate elements brutally into one force, a process fulfilled after the Korean war. Kim was born in 1912 and adopted the name of a former national hero. Imbued with passionate nationalism, Kim resolved to fight the Japanese and he became one of the intrepid guerrilla opponents of the Japanese army. During the 1930s Kim worked with the CCP. During the Pacific war he operated, in part, from bases in Soviet territory. Kim was regarded in the West, before and during the Korean war, as a Soviet puppet, but this was erroneous. Of necessity, Kim cooperated with the Soviet Union and with the CCP but he was nobody's puppet. Kim was determined to unite his country as soon as practicable and he believed that Korea should be guided by an ideology combining nationalism, communism and Korean features as he identified them. His intentions could not emerge too strongly at first, since Kim was dependent on the Soviet Union for patronage and support.

Why did Stalin put Kim into power at the head of a regime established by the Soviet Union [101]? The first reason is negative. Stalin had little faith in alternative candidates of whom the most conspicuous was Pak Hon-yong. Pak operated in Korea in underground activities under the Japanese and remained briefly in South Korea before moving to the north. Kim was young, vigorous, and not too deeply involved in the past factional disputes. Stalin regarded Kim as acceptable and no doubt controllable by Moscow. Land reform was applied rapidly in the north, facilitated by the fleeing southwards of many landowners. After a brief phase of limited toleration of non-communist leftists, the authority of the Workers Party was stamped ruthlessly on north Korea. The first signs of the later cult of Kim Il Sung began to emerge [18]. However, Kim was faced with much factionalism. Significant numbers of Koreans continued to fight in the CCP ranks during the Chinese civil war (1946–9). In 1949–50 many of them left China to join the army of the DPRK. Kim was also faced with rivalry from Pak Hon-yong who was better known than Kim. Kim's ardent wish to secure early unification of Korea may be interpreted as a move to strengthen his control of North Korea. The constitution of the DPRK was approved in July 1948 at a conference of the North Korean People's Council. Predictably Kim praised the generosity and friendship of the Soviet Union while castigating the duplicity of the United States. Pak Hon-yong took office as foreign minister, a post he held until the end of the Korean war when he was purged, tried for treason, found guilty and shot. Pak emphasised, and most likely exaggerated, the potential for spontaneous revolutionary developments in the south. It was in his interests to remind Kim and Stalin that rebellions in the south could be encouraged successfully. The rebellion in Cheju Island in October 1948 appeared to lend support to Pak's argument (a significant rising occurred in this remote island, promoted by traditional resentment of central authority and leftist agitation) [19, pp. 141–4].

The Soviet Union and China

Since the end of the Cold War, interesting evidence on the policies of the Soviet Union and China has materialised in the Soviet and Chinese archives. Much of this newly available evidence has been translated and sifted by scholars working in conjunction with the Woodrow Wilson International Center in Washington, DC [46]. The new evidence clarifies some aspects, but not all: certain Soviet and Chinese archives are still unavailable. However, crucial features are now clear. Kim Il Sung urged Stalin consistently to support armed action by the DPRK against the ROK. In March 1949 Kim led a delegation to Moscow in the course of which an economic and cultural agreement was concluded. Kim did not receive the support he sought for military action: Stalin was not convinced that the time was apposite. British observers regarded the North Korean forces as quite formidable and as being in the process of undergoing further strengthening through Soviet aid and through the return of Koreans fighting with the Chinese. Between January and April 1950 Stalin discarded his usual caution in international relations and changed course so as to support a North Korean offensive against the south (46; 102). Stalin's decision was indicated on 30 January 1950 when a change in direction occurred. Kim assured Stalin that he was confident of swift victory, without American intervention, when he visited Moscow in April 1950. Stalin reiterated that he did not want the situation in Korea to develop into a major crisis. Upon receiving the assurances he required, Stalin gave orders to the Soviet army to provide the aid and strategic assistance needed by Kim [46, p.87]. In May and June 1950 North Korean military plans were prepared jointly with the Soviet generals. Soviet military personnel with suitable battle expertise were sent to the DPRK to assist in the detailed planning.

Stalin's decision to support Kim's offensive has to be viewed in the light of Sino-Soviet relations [13; 110; 111]. In October 1949 Mao Tse-tung proclaimed the formal establishment of the People's

Republic of China [PRC]. A second great communist state now existed. Mao led the CCP to victory only fourteen years after assuming leadership of the party, in the midst of the Long March. He succeeded through redefining the strategy and direction of the CCP; this included placing heavy emphasis on the peasantry and on guerrilla warfare in addition to moving away from the past reliance on the Soviet Union. Mao respected the historic achievement of the Soviet party and what had been accomplished by Lenin and Stalin. But he held strongly that a communist party must discover its own path to success and that the Soviet Union must not dictate to China. Mao wanted to work with Russia; indeed, considering the economic problems facing China, it was imperative that the two communist giants should cooperate. Mao detested the United States and could discern no likelihood of *rapprochement* within the foreseeable future. Rather, rising anti–communist hysteria in the United States, plus ambiguous American intentions regarding Taiwan, propelled Mao into working with Stalin. Mao travelled to Moscow to meet Stalin in December 1949; he remained in Moscow for the unusual period of nearly seven weeks [60, p. 138].

The evidence concerning Mao's exchanges with Stalin reveals appreciable tension and friction [37, pp. 133–47, 215]. Stalin was determined to emphasise his seniority in the world revolutionary hierarchy and sometimes delayed seeing Mao or made critical observations on Mao's theoretical writings. Stalin possessed the trump card in that, at this juncture, Mao needed Stalin's help more than Stalin required his assistance. Eventually a series of Sino–Soviet agreements were signed on 14 February [46, pp. 5–9]. These included a treaty of friendship, alliance and assistance; specific agreements relating to Soviet interests in Manchuria arising from the agreements reached at the Yalta conference in February 1945; and Soviet economic aid. The treaty of alliance referred explicitly to the menace of revived Japanese militarism since the United States had implemented the 'reverse course' and was rebuilding Japan as a western bulwark in the Cold War [83]. Mao felt most passionately about the extended Russian presence in Manchuria. The agreement reached with Stalin provided for the return of the naval base at Port Arthur, and railway interests, by the end of 1952. Additional secret agreements were made, the full nature of which remain to be clarified. Reluctantly, China acknowledged the existence of Russian interests in Manchuria and Sinkiang that originated in the Tsarist era. Mao's ire emerged several years later when he complained to Molotov that Russia had treated China in the manner of imperialists in the past.

Mao was not intimately consulted by Stalin and Kim Il Sung regarding their preparations for the DPRK's advance against the ROK. Soviet assistance was important to Kim in prior planning, but neither he nor Stalin envisaged an active role for China. Kim visited Peking in May 1950 to inform Mao of developments. Mao favoured the elimination of the ROK and Korean unification, since this would deal a serious blow to American prestige. Mao resented his exclusion from the Stalin–Kim deliberations but he could only observe developments. Mao's immense pride and fervent belief in China's destiny meant that if the Korean war became a prolonged conflict, contrary to the wishes of Stalin and Kim, China probably would intervene. Mao was increasingly alienated from the United States because of the growing signs that the United States would intervene in the final stages of the Chinese civil war to deny possession of Taiwan to the PRC. This leads us back to considering the stance of the Truman administration on the eve of the start of the Korean war.

Taiwan and Korea

The future of Taiwan became a particularly delicate issue in the first half of 1950 and became linked with Korean developments [60, pp. 172–7]. Chiang Kai-shek and the defeated remnants of the Kuomintang retreated to Taiwan in 1949. Chiang intended remaining there for as long as possible, in the hope that the United States might decide to save him, perhaps just before the ominous chime at midnight. The Truman administration was wholly disillusioned with Chiang and wished to be rid of the Kuomintang. Large quantities of American aid had been sent to Chiang's regime and this had either fallen prey to endemic corruption in China or had been captured by the victorious communist forces. The triumph of communism in China became a highly controversial issue in American domestic politics because the Republican party, embittered at its fifth successive defeat in presidential elections in 1948, was using the failure of Truman's policy in China to assail the Democrats. In turn China fused with the acerbic atmosphere of McCarthyism and the hysterical hunt for the 'Reds' betraying the country from within [78]. Truman and Acheson did not want to intervene in Taiwan in order to rescue the moribund Kuomintang. However, wider considerations had to be addressed. The Pentagon argued that it was essential to prevent the PRC taking over Taiwan for strategic reasons. General MacArthur held this view vehemently [60, pp. 174–5]. As he contemplated the impact of the Cold War on Asia from the Dai Ichi building in Tokyo, MacArthur's hatred of the Chinese communists intensified. MacArthur regarded 'Red China' as a greater threat than the Soviet Union and he felt that urgent steps were required to block communist expansion. MacArthur believed that Taiwan was very important strategically and it was essential that the island should be denied to the PRC. The formal policy of the Truman administration was that the United States would not intervene in Taiwan, as Truman indicated in a statement issued in January 1950. Dean Acheson, the secretary of state, ideally would have welcomed an understanding with the PRC but he recognised that, because of the prevailing trends in Peking and Washington, this could not be achieved for years to come. Acheson inclined towards a form of neutralisation for Taiwan, possibly under the supervision of the UN, and the Taiwan autonomists might be assisted into power; the autonomists opposed the domination of Taiwan by mainlanders and wished to secure a government independent of both the Kuomintang and the communists [67]. Serious consideration was given in Washington to organising a coup in Taiwan to depose Chiang Kai-shek and to install a more pliable figure – the American-educated General Sun Li-jen was an obvious candidate [17, pp. 551–2, 562–7].

Therefore, on the eve of the outbreak of the Korean war, American policy on Taiwan was changing significantly to confirm that the PRC would not be allowed to invade Taiwan. Acheson conveyed this decision privately to the British ambassador in early June 1950, but knowledge was restricted to a small number of people in the State Department [60, pp. 175–6]. The first public acknowledgement came in President Truman's statement of 27 June 1950, following the start of fighting in Korea, when he said that the Seventh Fleet would act to stop the PRC invading Taiwan or the Kuomintang regime invading the mainland. Although Chiang often referred to this possibility, the former scenario was far more likely than the latter. The significance of Taiwan is twofold. It heightened tension and animosity between China and the United States. In addition, it revealed that the Truman administration was willing to adopt a tougher policy towards East Asia with the purpose of combating communism.

In June 1950 the situation in South Korea seemed much as usual. Syngman Rhee suffered a rebuff in elections held the previous month but he was not faced with a fundamental threat to his position. The economic indicators in the ROK worried the Americans, with inflation developing as a major problem. Rumblings along the 38th parallel continued, as in the preceding two years. John Foster Dulles, a Republican politician appointed by Truman and Acheson to handle the delicate negotiations for a Japanese peace treaty, visited Seoul in the middle of June. Dulles was *en route* to Tokyo to pursue discussions with MacArthur and the Japanese government relating to a peace treaty with Japan. It is likely that he visited Seoul so as to smooth over friction resulting from Rhee's annoyance at certain American statements made in the first half of 1950, notably the ambiguities inherent in Dean Acheson's National Press Club speech in January 1950 and, more particularly, Senator Tom Connally's unfortunate press interview in May in which Connally spoke pessimistically on the future of Korea. Dulles addressed the ROK national assembly on 19 June: he applauded Korea's emergence from the colonial era and emphasised that the American people welcomed the Koreans as an equal partner 'in the great company of those who comprised the free World' [60, p. 184]. In private Dulles told Rhee that it was imperative to construct a strong state in South Korea in which political and economic stability was secured. Dulles was impressed with the vigour displayed by the elderly ROK leader and told the British representative in Tokyo that Rhee would not prove supine and was capable of launching an attack against the DPRK. The statement caused some embarrassment in London where it was read shortly after the start of the war [61, p. 185].

On 22 June the British minister in Seoul resorted to the familiar British response when little was happening – he referred to the weather and welcomed the arrival of rain, which was badly needed [60, p. 185]. Captain Holt would soon have more serious problems to contemplate.

2

The Start of the War

On 25 June 1950 a coordinated North Korean offensive began and the forces of the DPRK advanced south. The North Korean forces were markedly better than their South Korean opponents in terms of numbers and experience. The DPRK army comprised approximately 100 000. Some had served with the Chinese Communist forces before and during the civil war; others had been trained by the Soviet army. The DPRK possessed significant air strength including fighters and light bombers. The ROK army lacked officers of sufficient experience, apart from those who had received training in the Japanese army. The American army mission (KMAG) had made only limited progress and certainly less than its head, General Roberts, claimed. The ROK had no aircraft and no tanks, principally because the Truman administration distrusted Rhee and feared that he might start a war if the ROK was given more aid.

The North Korean offensive was planned with extensive Soviet military assistance. Soviet personnel were conspicuous at the beginning of the war but once it became clear that the United States would respond vigorously and that the authority of the UN was being invoked, Stalin ordered the withdrawal of Soviet officers [46; 37]. The Soviet Union helped considerably in the background and was to play a major role in the air in supplying planes and personnel, but this was implemented covertly. Pilots were instructed not to converse in Russian and they did not wear Soviet uniforms.

The North Koreans revealed efficiency and tenacity in the pursuance of their advance. The ROK army reacted ineptly in the main, although individual units showed courage and dedication. The leadership and morale of the ROK army were poor and this was compounded by panic, such as the premature destruction of the Han bridge [29, part 1, p. 43]. Nearly half of the ROK army was on the other side when the bridge was destroyed. It was obvious that if South Korea did not receive outside assistance on a major scale, Kim Il Sung would become the ruler of the entire Korean peninsula.

21

Stalin and Kim had plotted on the assumption that the United States would not intervene on the Asian mainland. The confused American policy towards the ROK between 1948 and 1950 and the ambiguous character of Dean Acheson's National Press Club speech in January 1950 did not suggest that decisive American action was likely [1, pp. 354–8; 17, pp. 420–1]. However, Stalin was in possession of intelligence that should have alerted him to an alternative assessment [48, pp. 115, 174]. His spies included the British nationals, Donald Maclean, Guy Burgess and Kim Philby: they provided invaluable information on the trend of American policy-making. Maclean and Burgess worked in the Foreign Office and Maclean had served recently in a senior position in the British embassy in Washington. The most important development in American planning was National Security Council paper 68 – NSC 68 [17, pp. 625–30]. This was drafted early in 1950 and submitted to President Truman for approval in April 1950. This document emphasised that the United States must prepare itself for communist challenges, aimed at testing American morale and commitment anywhere in the world. Europe was the most vital area for American and western interests: the Berlin blockade constituted the most recent example of grave crisis in Europe and this culminated in victory for the West [86]. A future communist challenge could occur anywhere – in Asia or the Middle East. Such a challenge must be met immediately and firmly. Failure to respond would convey an image of weakness and would invite further threats, eventually weakening the West in Europe. The blunt message in NSC 68 was that greater resources should be devoted to defence and that western defences should be rendered more efficient.

Possibly Stalin regarded some of the intelligence he received as erroneous, planted to mislead or deceive. Stalin's extraordinarily suspicious nature, which was intensifying in the later 1940s, conceivably led him to doubt the reliability of some evidence produced by his agents. While the North Korean offensive rolled on, and it became clear that it would continue to progress for some weeks to come, political and diplomatic questions came to the fore [112, pp. 54–6, 62–4]. Here Stalin committed one egregious error: the Soviet Union did not participate in the deliberations of the UN Security Council. The Soviet delegate, Jacob Malik, had not attended the Security Council since January 1950 in protest at the refusal of the UN to seat a delegation from the PRC instead of continuing to recognise the Kuomintang regime of Chiang Kai-shek,

now confined to Taiwan and to other small islands off the coast of
China. The Soviet Foreign Ministry recommended that Malik
should return to his seat but Stalin overruled the recommendation.
It remains a mystery as to why Stalin responded as he did. One
possibility is that he wished to embroil the UN and the PRC so as
to postpone any chance of a *rapprochement* between the United
States and China. If Stalin did respond in this way, then he should
have assessed the repercussions of allowing the UN to be used by
the United States as a more convenient way of persuading democratic opinion in the world to accept the legitimacy of American
intervention in Korea. Another explanation is that Stalin did not
believe that the United States would act militarily and by the time
he awoke to reality, it was too late to reverse the damage done. One
is reminded of Talleyrand's mordant observation – 'worse than a
crime, a mistake'.

American reactions

When news reached Washington of the North Korean attack, senior
American leaders and officials were absent from the capital. Truman
was at home in Independence, Missouri. Acheson was at his farm in
Maryland. However, American reactions were surprisingly swift and
decisive. Acheson returned swiftly to Washington and took the
immediate decision to convene an emergency meeting of the UN
Security Council and to secure condemnation of the DPRK, with a
demand for a return to the *status quo ante*. Acheson spoke to
Truman by telephone and the president approved the action taken
by the secretary of state [60, pp. 186–8]. The Security Council carried
a resolution on 25 June registering that a breach of the peace had
occurred, condemning the North Korean attack and calling for
peace to be restored. In Tokyo General MacArthur initially
regarded news of the developments in Korea as yet another of the
many incidents which had occurred in the vicinity of the 38th
parallel during the preceding two years. John Foster Dulles, who
was in Tokyo to pursue discussions relating to a Japanese peace
treaty, alerted MacArthur to the reality, since he had been in Seoul a
week before and he appreciated that the crisis was grave. MacArthur
subsequently authorised the dispatch of aid to the ROK before he
received formal permission from Washington – an early example of
MacArthur's inclination to act independently [49, p. 420].

Truman met his principal colleagues and advisers upon his return to Washington. The Pentagon held that American air power should be deployed so as to eliminate North Korean tanks and to slow down the advance of the DPRK army. The Pentagon and the secretary for defense, Louis Johnson, hoped to avoid committing ground forces in Korea. It was agreed that the Seventh Fleet should be sent to the China Sea with the intention of preventing an invasion of Taiwan by PRC forces. It was important to encourage support from other western states and a British offer of naval assistance was welcomed; the Seventh Fleet was not in the region and the United States could not bring naval power immediately to bear, so the British response was most helpful. It should be noted that the British view of Taiwan was different from that of the United States. Britain recognised the PRC in January 1950 and believed that Taiwan should eventually come under the control of Peking [59].

The response of governments in western Europe and in the Commonwealth was that communist aggression must be condemned but there was reluctance to contemplate a large-scale military involvement in Korea. Understandably European countries saw themselves as in the front line of resistance to Soviet expansion: Europe was the core of the Cold War as it was developing. To become involved deeply in Korea could represent a dangerous diversion from Europe. Some American politicians, particularly in the Republican party, argued that Europe was given excessive attention and that Asia should be accorded greater priority [11; 3]. This was the emphatic opinion of MacArthur who was likely to loom larger on the scene before long. Political realities dictated that the United States must be supported otherwise American enthusiasm for defending western Europe could decline. It was essential that public opinion in the democracies should understand the Korean war as a fundamental threat to the principles underpinning the UN Charter. This meant that the UN, as an organisation, should be committed as fully as possible, although most of the resources would come from the United States.

The military situation in Korea deteriorated rapidly as South Korean resistance crumbled. The Security Council met on 27 June and carried by seven votes to one an American resolution that the members of the UN should oppose North Korean aggression and extend appropriate support to the ROK. The Attlee government in Britain fully supported the resolution but felt that British troops should not be committed to action in Korea [59, pp. 191–2, 196]. British commitments in Germany, the Middle East and Malaya were so extensive that the addition of a further major responsibility would place extreme burdens on the British budget and on British defence capabilities. The chiefs of staff were wholly willing to see the existing strength of the Royal Navy present in East Asian waters deployed to help the UN.

The extent of the North Korean advance in late June meant that the hopes entertained at first in the Pentagon that air power might suffice in slowing or halting the North Korean offensive were shown to be fallacious. Graver decisions had to be made. Douglas MacArthur became the key military actor in determining UN responses. He visited Korea on 30 June and provided a bleak assessment [49]. The ROK army could not cope with the demands placed upon it, which were far bigger than anticipated up until 25 June. The only way to block the North Koreans and to ensure that communism did not prevail throughout the Korean peninsula was to introduce American troops. It was impossible to proceed solely with air and naval power.

The Truman administration rose to the challenge, holding that it faced no choice. Truman regarded events in Korea as a flagrant challenge to the free world, fulfilling the prophetic statements contained in NSC 68. It was the biggest test of his presidency and he believed that it must be faced regardless of the consequences [60, pp. 186–8]. The United States must move firmly to deploy American troops and forces provided by other UN member states. Truman wished to use the authority and prestige of the UN but without ceding independence of decision-making to the UN. The latter would do what the United States decided and not the reverse. Truman wanted to avoid disputes with the American Congress and for this reason did not request a congressional declaration of war. The president defined the operations in Korea as 'police action' under the UN flag. This allowed him freedom of manoeuvre but without risking Republican censure that he had permitted the UN to decide American policy. Since many Republicans had urged vociferously that more should be done to contain communism, it was difficult and unpatriotic to object when the president acted to do so. Senator Robert A. Taft, Sr, of Ohio, the leading right-wing contender for the Republican presidential nomination in 1952, complained that Congress should have been consulted, an important constitutional point which acquires more significance in the light of the policies towards the Vietnam war pursued by Presidents Kennedy, Johnson and Nixon. In late June and July 1950 Harry Truman was well-placed to rally the American people, given the desperate situation in the Korean peninsula. He used his power effectively as he advanced into an upward curve in the fortunes of his administration before the long decline which set in from November 1950.

The United Nations Command

The most urgent immediate decision was to appoint the head of the United Nations Command [UNC]. It was imperative to announce the appointment rapidly in order to organise the counter-attack and to encourage other members of the UN to contribute: if the UN flag was to have real meaning, it was necessary to persuade as many member states as possible to participate [62, p. 243]. There was one obvious and, in one sense, outstanding candidate – Douglas MacArthur. He was the greatest living American soldier with a highly distinguished record stretching back throughout the first half of the century. MacArthur had served in the expeditionary force to France in 1917–18; he had been commandant at West Point and chief of staff of the army; he had then served as defence adviser to the Philippines before the Japanese attack, before assuming command in the south-west Pacific from 1942 to 1945; finally, he held office as SCAP in Japan following Japan's surrender. Much of MacArthur's career was spent in Asia and he regarded himself as a great authority on Asia [49; 81]. He was a man of diverse talents and contradictions. Often sweeping and sometimes original in his appraisals, MacArthur was also vain and too prone to placing himself and his judgement on a remote pedestal. MacArthur was not simply an outstanding general: he was a political general in more ways than one. As his record during the Pacific war demonstrated, he was prepared to be unscrupulous in exerting pressure on the White House via his friends in Congress and to threaten direct political involvement. He was a supporter of the Republican party and was identified with its rising right wing. MacArthur was not a typical Republican: his idiosyncratic character precluded such a definition being applied. As SCAP in Japan MacArthur sponsored a number of liberal or radical reforms and was criticised by some Republicans for supporting 'socialistic' measures [7, pp. 41–141; 83, pp. 11–197]. He deeply resented such criticism which he regarded as ill–informed, prejudiced and sometimes denoting the views of vested interests. MacArthur possessed one major ambition: he wished to become president of the United States. He was a possible choice for the Republication nomination in 1944 and 1948, more obviously on the latter occasion. His candidacy faltered and then collapsed for several reasons. MacArthur remained in Japan and would not return to the United States to campaign personally; his supporters comprised a combination of reactionary and progressive Republicans, but they were ill-organised and insufficiently cohesive; MacArthur's rivals revealed more dexterity and aptitude. MacArthur's hopes of gaining the nomination in a deadlocked convention evaporated when the Republicans nominated Governor Thomas E. Dewey of New York for a second time. Despite his disappointment, MacArthur still entertained one last opportunity of gaining the nomination in 1952. The Republicans would want a tough, charismatic candidate in order to end twenty years of Democratic occupation of the White House. MacArthur had proved a successful, flexible and sometimes remarkably enlightened reformer in Japan. Defeating a communist offensive in Asia and rolling back the 'Red menace' in Korea could prove an irresistible appeal in an impressive curriculum vitae. Douglas MacArthur desperately wanted to become head of UNC in addition to retaining his existing posts in Japan.

The arguments in favour of his appointment were clear enough. The arguments against were quite persuasive too. MacArthur was seventy years of age in 1950 and he had not conducted a military campaign since 1945. He had reached an age where a certain slowing down had to be expected. Was he really capable of enduring the profound strains of directing complex military operations in a most challenging environment? Beyond this occurred the question of his preference for acting independently. Neither Franklin Roosevelt nor Harry Truman liked or trusted MacArthur, yet each recognised his ability and appointed him to high office. The dangers were manifest and were emphasised at the beginning of the Korean war by the secretary for defense, Louis Johnson, when he warned, perceptively, that MacArthur should not be allowed freedom to interpret directives as he wished [60, p. 188]. Probably two factors influenced Truman's decision to appoint MacArthur: he was already based in East Asia and he was a Republican in domestic politics. A bipartisan approach would be advanced through appointing a

Republican at the head of American and UN operations. It would be more difficult for the Republican party to criticise MacArthur and it might render criticism of the UN more difficult. So MacArthur was appointed and commenced the challenging task of preparing the UN counter-attack. At first he would have to rely on American troops from Japan, many of whom were ill-prepared for the abrupt transition from a relatively luxurious lifestyle in Japan to the rigours of a daunting campaign in Korea. Strong pressure was brought to bear by Dean Acheson to convince America's allies to contribute forces to Korea. In Britain the Attlee government was reluctant to send troops for reasons discussed earlier. However, American pressure was so strong that the Attlee government gave way and agreed late in July to dispatch troops including 'national servicemen' (young men undergoing compulsory military service) [59, pp. 192–4; 70, pp. 422–4].

In total, fifteen countries joined the United States in extending military, air or naval assistance for the campaigns in Korea – Australia, Belgium, Canada, Colombia, Ethiopia, France, Greece, Luxembourg, the Netherlands, New Zealand, the Philippines, Thailand, Turkey, the Union of South Africa and the United Kingdom. Medical units were supplied by Denmark, Italy, India, Norway and Sweden. MacArthur was appointed formally following the passage of a resolution by the UN Security Council on 7 July 1950, carried by seven votes to none against with three abstentions. The resolution reiterated determination to terminate communist aggression and urged members to assist; the United States was requested to appoint a commander-in-chief. MacArthur's new appointment was in addition to his existing appointments as SCAP and as head of American forces in Japan.

The North Korean offensive

In contemplating the magnitude of the military problems facing the UNC, it is necessary to look at Map 3 and remind ourselves of the character of the North Korean attack. The ROK capital, Seoul, fell to the enemy within three days of the start of the war. Syngman Rhee and the American ambassador, John J. Muccio, retreated south; the unfortunate British minister, Captain Vyvyan Holt, remained in Seoul and was compelled to accept the rigours of being

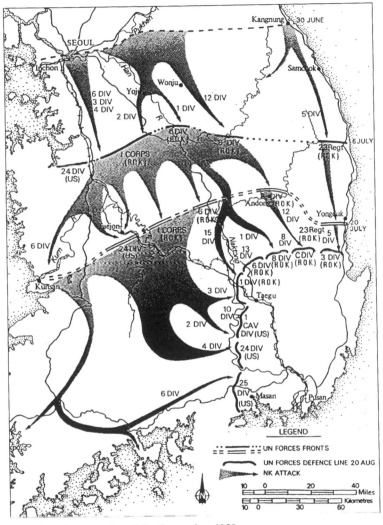

Map 3   *The campaign, July–September 1950*

a prisoner of the DPRK. Holt was accompanied into captivity by a colleague, George Blake, head of local British intelligence who soon became, if he was not already, a communist agent [59, pp. 186, 189n.95]. On 30 June the ROK army line lay south of Seoul. MacArthur could conduct only a holding operation pending the arrival of more men and resources. On 15 July the UNC's line extended from just above Yongdok in the east to just below Kunsan in the west. The UNC was forced to retreat further in August, back to what became known as the 'Pusan redoubt', that is, a fairly small part of south-east Korea from just below An'gang-si and Tabu to the major port of Pusan in the far south. The western press and other media supplied breathless, excited reports on the grim struggle to their readers or listeners. The Cold War had developed into a desperate hot war, fought in an obscure Asian peninsula.

As they advanced, the DPRK forces sought to punish supporters of the ROK, often savagely. The behaviour of the DPRK and the ROK forces and agents, during the sharp variations in fortunes between June and November 1950, reminds us that the Korean conflict was a shocking civil war in which the victors showed no mercy in torturing and murdering men, women and children. The North Korean army proved efficient and ruthless. However, General Farrar-Hockley has pointed out that if Kim had concentrated upon capturing the south-east, instead of the south-west, in the second half of July, 'he might have won the war in a mighty manoeuvre of encirclement' by advancing on Pusan through Chinju [29, part 1, p. 132]. MacArthur appointed Lieutenant-General Walton H. Walker as head of the Eighth Army. The ROK army was reorganised as part of the process of restoring morale and confidence. American forces would bear the brunt, as there was no likelihood of the ROK army becoming very effective in the near future. During July the North Koreans moved forward by between ten and fifteen miles a day, which was a creditable rate of advance. It was essential for the UNC to retain control of south-east Korea: the alternative would be evacuation of the peninsula, which would be a profound humiliation. MacArthur and Walker sought to instil the requisite determination into the American troops [20, part 1, pp. 130–5]. Walker had approximately 33 000 troops under his command in the third week of July. Reinforcements materialised at the end of the month with marines and infantry arriving on 30 and 31 July. The American troops launched a counter-attack from the lower Naktong river, from Waegwan to Taegu, and along the east coast. Kim Il Sung urged the NKPA to complete its offensive speedily but Walker's success in motivating the American forces led to a stabilisation in the UNC. The Naktong crossings were regained on 19 August. Meanwhile, the first British troops reached Pusan at the end of August.

Pressure was mounting on the NKPA by late August. Losses climbed to approximately 60 000 by the end of the first week of August. Captured South Koreans were conscripted to serve, which meant that the NKPA strength in fighting terms stood at around 68 000. The United States forces engaged in fighting totalled around 35 000 officers and men. The ROK army totalled approximately 73 000, having incurred losses of around 70 000 [30, pp. 137–8]. American air action had a significant effect in reducing the NKPA's ability to deliver supplies but not to the point where the NKPA's capacity to attack was halted. Renewed serious fighting broke out at the end of August and in the first two days of September in the region of Masan and across the lower and then upper Naktong. However, the situation in the first week of September was that Kim Il Sung's optimism that his forces would have liquidated the ROK and expelled the UNC from the peninsula by this time had been thwarted decisively. The strains on the NKPA were growing daily, just as reinforcements for the UNC were accumulating. MacArthur and Walker had surmounted the extreme peril of late July and early August. Shortly the Korean war would move into its next phase in which the tables would be turned on the DPRK.

The Role of the United Nations

Before considering military developments further in the next chapter, it is relevant to discuss international diplomatic issues. The Korean war constituted the first major challenge to the UN. The secretary-general, Trygve Lie, was an amiable Norwegian, supported originally by the Soviet Union: by 1950 Russia lost confidence in him, deeming him too sympathetic to western viewpoints. Lie believed that the UN had obligations in Korea in consequence of the activities of two UN commissions (UNTCOK and UNCOK) [62, pp. 140, 349–50]. UN observers were present in Korea and visited the vicinity of the 38th parallel shortly before the DPRK attack. Two Australian military observers represented UNCOK, Major F. S. B. Peach and Squadron-Leader R. J. Rankin. Between 9 and 23 June they inspected ROK troops, stationed along the 38th parallel. They reported that ROK forces were deployed defensively and were in no position to launch an offensive to the north [60, pp. 178–9]. While some movement of civilians had occurred to the north of the parallel, there was no indication that a North

Korean offensive was imminent. The report from Peach and Rankin was sent to UNCOK on 24 June and led UNCOK to conclude, in the light of events on 25 June, that the DPRK was responsible for implementing aggression against the ROK. Trygve Lie and the UN secretariat in New York concluded that the UN charter had been breached and that a firm response was essential if the UN's authority was to mean anything. The UN could only be as strong as its leading members were prepared to make it and in this particular context only one power counted. Once the United States decided to act, the UN would be associated with it, assuming that the Soviet delegate did not return to the Security Council in order to veto action. When this hurdle was surmounted with the continuing absence of Malik, the UN was committed. The UN secretariat would have liked more information and certainly greater consultation than occurred. The Truman administration did not wish to restrict its independence through accepting greater commitments to the UN in New York than was basically required. At the beginning of the war, a widespread feeling of grave crisis manifested itself among UN members, even among those who entertained doubts over American foreign policy. Jawaharlal Nehru, the prime minister of India, condemned North Korea and believed that aggression must be deterred and punished. But Nehru came rapidly to resent what he perceived as an arrogant, overbearing and bullying American attitude to members of the UN who wished to express reservations or criticism concerning American policy. Of course, Nehru wished to develop a distinct role for India as a leader of the emerging third world, particularly in Asia [89; 38]. The United States regarded Nehru's criticisms of American conduct as negative and carping. India's ability to communicate with the Chinese government via its ambassador in Peking, K. M. Panikkar, was viewed with suspicion in Washington as regards the kind of reports forwarded by Panikkar to New Delhi. This will be discussed further in the next chapter.

The member states of the UN supporting the American-led intervention regarded the action taken by the DPRK on 25 June 1950 as a grave breach of the UN Charter. In so viewing the situation, they underestimated the fact that what occurred in June 1950 was a continuation of a civil war that began in 1945, if not earlier, and which was exacerbated by the action of the United States and the Soviet Union. Anxiety grew among UN members over the reluctance of the United States to consult meaningfully and significant examples will be given in later chapters. The dilemma for UN members was that those in Europe and in the 'old Commonwealth' (Canada, Australia, New Zealand and, although diminishingly, the Union of South Africa) required American support and could not afford to alienate the United States. Therefore, the atmosphere was one of ambivalence and tension: the latter was sometimes hidden and sometimes overt.

The Soviet Union, the United States and Britain

Finally, we need to consider the curious position of the Soviet Union in June–August 1950 and the differences between the American and British responses to the Soviet role. Stalin took the fateful decision earlier in 1950 to support Kim Il Sung's request to unify Korea by force. But this was on condition that a major crisis did not ensue. Once it became clear that the Truman administration would act firmly and would utilise the UN as part of this reaction, Stalin was faced with a dangerous situation which could escalate into a third world war. Stalin was not ready for such an eventuality in 1950, although he considered another world war to be likely later in the 1950s; the Soviet Union would not be prepared for war until 1955–6. Immediately after the war started, the Soviet Union adopted the same public stance as the DPRK in justifying its military action. South Korea had created an inflammatory situation and had attacked first [60, pp. 191–2]. However, there was no indication that the Soviet Union would intervene militarily in reaction to the United States and UN. Most American politicians and officials believed that the Soviet Union was entirely responsible for the outbreak of war, underestimating Kim's capacity for cajoling Stalin to lend Soviet support. The prevailing view in the British Foreign Office and among the majority of British politicians was that the Soviet Union had probably directed and orchestrated the DPRK's advance. But it was felt in London that the dangers of escalation must be recognised and that Stalin should be permitted an opportunity to retreat or at least modify the Soviet stance rather than being pushed further towards supporting Kim Il Sung [59, pp. 194–7]. The British foreign secretary, Ernest Bevin, was in poor health and was recuperating from an operation when the war began. Bevin was kept informed and wanted to use diplomacy to ease the crisis and, if possible, end it. Initially it proved impossible to contact the deputy Soviet foreign minister, Andrei Gromyko, but the latter reappeared in Moscow at the end of June and adopted a conciliatory approach in meetings with the British and American ambassadors. The aim was to persuade the Soviet Union to restore the *status quo ante*.

Attlee and Bevin sought to persuade the Truman administration to follow a path of compromise. Britain disapproved of the linking of Taiwan with Korea in Truman's public statement of 27 June. Issues concerning China should be separated from those concerning Korea. The PRC should be represented in the UN instead of Chiang Kai-shek's regime in Taiwan and the fate of Taiwan itself should come under the authority of the Peking government. The Truman administration was highly sensitive on matters relating to Taiwan and Chinese representation in the UN for political and strategic reasons. Each was controversial in domestic politics while the Pentagon and MacArthur emphasised that Taiwan must be kept out of communist hands. Thus Bevin's attitude in early July, in communicating his opinions candidly, upset Dean Acheson. The latter made clear that he was not prepared to make significant concessions [59, pp. 196–7]. Acheson argued that the Soviet Union had started the crisis and misjudged American and UN reactions. Communism was a global menace and communist rebellions were serious in South-East Asia. American policy on China would not change; the future of Taiwan needed to be decided on a basis that would connote stability and without the PRC establishing itself in Taiwan. Stalin could perceive the differences between the United States and Britain clearly enough but it was equally obvious that Britain could not dissuade the United States and that the Attlee government could not risk a fundamental rift in Anglo-American relations. As he observed developments [46; 103], Stalin's natural caution in the international sphere reasserted itself in July. He decided to avoid direct signs of Soviet intervention in Korea; Soviet aid would continue to support the DPRK and, if necessary, China could be encouraged to participate. For the present it was best to resume Soviet attendance in the Security Council. It would be foolish to allow the United States to develop further its dominance in the Security Council. It was the Soviet Union's turn to chair the Security Council in fulfilment of the customary principle of rotation. This would force the United States to use the General Assembly to advance its interests. Stalin could not reverse the damage done through formal UN commitment in Korea but he could provide checks and cause obstruction. Jacob Malik duly returned to chair the Security Council on 1 August 1950 and the following month was filled with acrimonious, mutually vituperative propaganda exchanges between Malik and the American delegate, Warren Austin [60, pp. 210–11].

As regards China, the PRC pursued a watching role. Official statements blamed South Korea and confirmed Chinese support for the 'progressive forces' led by Comrade Kim Il Sung. There was no immediate indication of Chinese action extending beyond rhetoric. The Indian ambassador in Peking reported that the PRC was interested primarily in Taiwan, but once the tide turned in Korea and the DPRK was forced to retreat, so China would have to decide how it was going to respond [60, p. 216].

Therefore, all hinged on the UN military operations in Korea and how General MacArthur envisaged avenging the reverses suffered by the UN and the ROK in the preceding two months.

3
China Enters the Conflict

In the middle of September 1950 the UNC transformed the character of the Korean war with the landing at Inchon. When MacArthur was appointed, he was fully confident that he could reverse the successes achieved by the audacious North Koreans, provided that he could retain the Pusan redoubt and that sufficient resources were made available. The port of Inchon, situated approximately midway on the western coast of the peninsula, near to Seoul, was an obvious attraction to a general seeking to launch a decisive counter-attack. This required a combined naval–military operation to attack the enemy in the rear and thus, at a stroke, to deprive Kim Il Sung's forces of the initiative possessed so far. There were problems as well as advantages in choosing Inchon: the tide varies by over thirty feet daily. Tides could be treacherous and necessitated accurate timing and skill with a significant measure of luck, which is always impossible to quantify. MacArthur wished to land 70 000 troops plus equipment. The joint chiefs of staff in Washington were uneasy at the scale of such a landing in hazardous conditions but acquiesced in MacArthur's preference. The Inchon landing was the result of genuinely representative UNC cooperation: American, Australian, British, Canadian, Dutch and French ships worked in unison with the addition of ROK vessels. The troops were landed swiftly and North Korean defenders were defeated or withdrew [29, p. 152]. UNC forces launched counter-attacks to break out of the Pusan redoubt so as to force back the NKPA, weaken its morale and secure the upper hand while political decisions were reached on the future of Korea. The fortunes of war switched, in the course of the second half of September, as speedily as had been the case with the successful offensive of the NKPA, three months before. By 30 September American and ROK forces

were approaching the 38th parallel and Seoul was liberated.
MacArthur presided triumphantly at a ceremony in which Syngman Rhee celebrated the success of the UNC. North Korean
remnants remained, notably in the south–west and east, to be
mopped up subsequently [29, part 1, map, opposite p. 159].

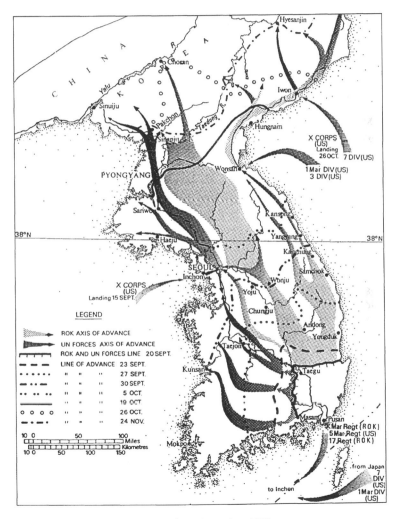

Map 4   *The campaign, September–November 1950*

Rollback

MacArthur accomplished all that could be expected of him by the end of September and his reputation rose as rapidly as it was to decline two months later. The United States and the UN now faced fundamental political decisions which were even more profound than many appreciated at the time. What were the aims of the UN? Were UNC forces to advance north of the 38th parallel and, if so, were they to proceed to the Yalu and the borders with China and the Soviet Union? What were the dangers in such an approach and were these dangers evaluated adequately? There was uncertainty over UN aims once aggression had been rebuffed. When UN forces reached the 38th parallel, the areas conquered by the DPRK were restored to the ROK. As an organisation, the UN was pledged to secure the unification of Korea under the terms of the resolutions carried by the General Assembly in 1947–8. The UN was committed to obtaining this objective peacefully, but once the DPRK employed force, it could be argued that the UN was entitled to authorise the forces acting in its name to implement unification. There were strong pressures upon political leaders, officials and generals to fulfil this policy, regardless of the opposition. UN success in Korea would be a powerful vindication of the principles represented in the UN Charter. Furthermore, it would constitute an important defeat for communism and a great victory for the 'free world'. The concept of 'rollback' thus emerged in a Korean context [19, pp. 4–5, 9–11, 26–7, 29–38, 49–53; 49, pp. 486–517]. Most American officials believed that rollback should be applied: the communists started the war and no concessions should be made to them. To halt at the 38th parallel or to move only a short distance into North Korea would be craven and could give the DPRK the opportunity to recover, threatening renewed warfare. MacArthur held fervently that Korea must be unified through the elimination of the DPRK; of course, he had his own political reasons, apart from strategic reasons, for favouring this approach [49, pp. 486–517]. Truman and Acheson were attracted by rollback because it seemed to promise a clear-cut solution and one that might lead to large dividends for an administration that had incurred heavy criticism from its domestic opponents for alleged weakness and incompetence in meeting the communist threat in Asia.

British leaders reacted in a not dissimilar way, although more divisions existed among officials. Attlee and Bevin did not face the kind of mordant censure over foreign policy from domestic opponents as was experienced by Truman and Acheson. The Attlee government had given a clear lead in warning of the great importance of organising and mobilising the West against perceived communist expansion [10; 70]. Admittedly this arose primarily in the context of Europe but anxiety over Asia grew in 1948–9 in the light of the instability and communist rebellions occurring in South–East Asia. The UN mission in Korea should be fulfilled by advancing beyond the 38th parallel. Officials in the Foreign Office essentially concurred, although some concern existed arising from the reports forwarded by the Indian government, based on information from Panikkar. The principal scepticism and then opposition to moving north came from the British chiefs of staff [61, pp. 631–6]. They warned perceptively that it was not essential to advance to the far north of Korea: it might be desirable to move a short way beyond the 38th parallel and then stop, but it would be dangerous to risk the possibility that China might enter into the war. Of the three chiefs of staff – Field Marshal Sir William Slim, Admiral Lord Fraser of North Cape, and Marshal of the Royal Air Force Sir John Slessor – Slessor was the most concerned, the most persistent in expressing criticism and the ablest. He was critical of the ROK government and castigated Rhee's approach to Korean unification which was hardly compatible with the ideals expressed in the UN Charter [59, p. 202]. Slessor held that there was a definite danger that China might intervene and the more provocative were the statements emanating from MacArthur and others in authority in Washington, the more real this threat would become. The Attlee cabinet disregarded this warning in October and agreed that Britain should act as cosponsor of a UN resolution in the General Assembly on 7 October, authorising the crossing of the 38th parallel by UNC forces. Later in October opinion changed and Britain recommended the creation of a buffer zone within North Korea with the purpose of allaying Chinese apprehension [28]. The response in Washington was unenthusiastic and MacArthur rejected such views categorically.

Unease over the future developed, especially among more liberal opinion in countries contributing to the UN operations, because of the conduct of the ROK government and its agents. How was Korea to be governed and what criteria should be laid down? Many Americans regarded Syngman Rhee as a hero of resistance to communism, which in one sense he was. Rhee was a man of passionate conviction and commitment who had worked throughout his career to secure a unified Korea. He wished to see an end to foreign intervention in Korea but he recognised that circumstances necessitated American and UN presence. Rhee was also wholly unscrupulous, ruthless, intolerant of criticism and prepared to use extremely repressive action to consolidate his rule [18, pp. 221–4]. Rhee believed Korea should be unified under his leadership and control. Those who had supported communism, flirted with communism or expressed opposition to Rhee's rule deserved no sympathy and should be punished suitably. The Korean conflict was in part a civil war. Kim Il Sung's approach resembled Rhee's in a number of respects, not least in treating opponents or possible opponents with great rigour and brutality. Atrocities were committed by the NKPA, just as they were by ROK forces and Rhee's agents. The western press began to report in late September and October the meting out of retribution by Rhee's regime. Louis Heren in *The Times* and James Cameron in *Picture Post* were prominent in revealing the methods used by agents of the ROK [59, p. 203; 42, p. 92]. Cameron's prose was complemented by the photographs of Bert Hardy, depicting shaven-headed men awaiting beating, torture or execution. The degradation of war was conveyed graphically. This did not harmonise with the stirring rhetoric of liberation reiterated by the American and British governments and the UN. Sir John Slessor was one who was appalled by revelations of Rhee's ideas of how Koreans should be treated and he warned that Korea should not be unified in such a way as to permit Rhee even more freedom to 'misgovern' Korea [59, p. 203]. Many members of the Labour and Liberal parties in Britain and some Conservatives contended that the liberation of Korea from communism should not result in the imposition of a dictatorial right-wing regime bellowing patriotic verbiage. The UN was committed to holding elections to secure unification in a manner desired by the Korean people. Britain emphasised that the UN must encourage genuine choice and not act as a rubber stamp for Rhee's ambition. The United States was less critical of Rhee while deploring excesses.

Truman meets MacArthur

The future character of the government of Korea remained to be determined once MacArthur's military operations advanced further north. In mid-October Truman flew to Wake Island in the western Pacific to meet MacArthur. It was the first meeting between the two men and occurred amidst some tension and mutual suspicion [60, pp. 226–9; 49, pp. 500–17]. MacArthur distrusted Truman and regarded him with a certain contempt. Truman fully reciprocated, seeing MacArthur as a general too obsessed with his own ego. It is probable that Truman wished to test MacArthur's opinion and judgement with reference to possible intervention by the Soviet Union or China as the UNC drove north. MacArthur discounted the likelihood of either intervening. American air superiority was a powerful factor discouraging Chinese action. The Chinese were building their military strength in Manchuria but MacArthur did not regard a Chinese threat as serious. There were no signs that Russia was contemplating action. The Soviet Union was quite formidable in the air and, indeed, Russian planes and pilots were to make a significant contribution, short of formal Soviet action. In all, MacArthur appeared confident but, in retrospect, complacent. Truman's visit ensured that if matters went wrong in Korea, then MacArthur's responsibility would be clear.

Stalin and Mao

MacArthur was correct in one respect but crucially wrong in the other respect. The Soviet Union would not intervene directly but would be substantially involved indirectly. He was entirely mistaken in his assessment of China's role. At this point it is essential to consider the evidence which has emerged since the end of the Cold War concerning the relationship between the Soviet Union and China in October 1950 and the Chinese decision to act militarily. Mao Tse-tung observed developments in Korea with growing anxiety in September 1950 as it became clear that the DPRK was experiencing a grave and potentially devastating counter-attack [13; 111]. Mao was annoyed that he had not been consulted properly by Stalin and Kim Il Sung before the NKPA offensive began on 25 June. He was irate with the United States for its provocative action over Taiwan and regarded the onward march of American troops under the UN flag as dangerous and insulting. Vital Chinese interests were at stake and Mao believed that China would have to intervene in order to stop American imperialism advancing further in the Asian continent. American agents were encouraging opposition to Mao's government in scattered border areas of China and were assisting Kuomintang remnants and other dissidents. If MacArthur's forces reached the Manchurian border, the United States would be well-placed to interfere in a key economic region. Furthermore, Mao was determined to assert China's regained sovereignty and not to fall back into accepting foreign imperialism in China. However, nobody could doubt the magnitude of the decision confronting Mao and his colleagues [46].

Stalin wanted China to act and indicated that he would extend appreciable support. Chinese leaders met early in October to decide on the next step and to review the challenges facing them. Deep concern was felt by the majority. Chou En-lai and Lin Piao both opposed intervention on the grounds that too many risks were involved and that the war would prove too big a strain for the fragile economy, which was recovering from decades of war and internal conflict [37, p. 180]. Mao argued firmly that China must act and accept the consequences. He was supported by P'eng Teh-huai, a courageous general who was shortly to assume command of the Chinese 'volunteers' in Korea. Given China's weakness in the air, it was imperative to secure Soviet assistance in the air. Chou En-lai was dispatched to Moscow to consult Stalin [37, p. 189]. There is some divergence between evidence in the Russian and Chinese archives regarding undertakings given (or not given) by Stalin [37, p. 189]. Chinese historians have stated that Stalin gave a firm promise to Chou that Soviet air action would be overt and that Mao regarded this as fundamental to Chinese intervention; subsequently Stalin decided against direct action because this would be too dangerous and could lead to full Soviet participation in the war. Soviet sources indicate that Stalin did not give a binding commitment and that Chou was misled by the ambiguous nature of Stalin's remarks [46]. At any rate, Stalin's response was disappointing and humiliating to Mao. Some sources suggest that Mao suffered a temporary breakdown on receiving the news. The Chinese leaders nevertheless, under Mao's powerful urging, decided that China must intervene and the orders were given for troop movements to proceed prior to the advance of Chinese forces into Korea. P'eng Teh-huai was designated commander after Lin Piao declined on grounds of ill health: the latter was genuine but Lin had made clear that he was opposed to Chinese intervention.

We need now to remind ourselves of the progress north of UNC forces. A resolution carried in the UN General Assembly on 7 October created a new body to replace UNCOK. This was termed the United Nations Commission for the Unification and Rehabilitation of Korea (UNCURK). The new body was charged with implementing the UN's policy of a unified, democratic government for all of Korea and to address issues of relief and rehabilitation. The membership of UNCURK comprised Australia, Chile, the Netherlands, Pakistan, the Philippines, Thailand and Turkey. China condemned the establishment of UNCURK. American troops crossed the 38th parallel on 7 October, ROK troops having crossed earlier. MacArthur made two broadcasts urging the DPRK to cease military operations. On 9 October MacArthur stated:

> In order that the decisions of the United Nations may be carried out with a minimum of further loss of life and destruction of property, I, as the United Nations Commander-in-Chief, for the last time call upon you and the forces under your command in whatever part of Korea situated, to lay down your arms and cease hostilities. And I call upon all north Koreans to co-operate fully with the United Nations in establishing a unified, independent and democratic government of Korea, assured that they will be treated justly and that the United Nations will act to relieve and rehabilitate all parts of a unified Korea. [29, part 1, p. 230]

Kim Il Sung regarded this statement with defiant contempt. There is evidence of dissent within the higher levels of the DPRK, following the savage reversal of fortunes which had just occurred. Apparently, approaches were made to Mao Tse-tung at the end of September to support the removal of Kim Il Sung but Mao refused: to depose Kim would be to remove a strong leader, if one with considerable defects in judgement, and would exacerbate the problems facing the retreating North Korean administration [13, p. 162].

While defeated, the NKPA was not disintegrating. Bruce Cumings has observed that the NKPA remained formidable and the speed of its retreat occurred in part to facilitate regrouping in the north-west [17, pp. 740, 744; 29, part 1, map, opposite p. 235]. Unless Kim Il Sung complied with the terms stipulated in his broadcast, MacArthur was determined to apply the advance northwards as fast as he could so as to fulfil his desire to end the war before Christmas. He underestimated the continued or revivified fighting capacity of the NKPA and, most importantly, brushed aside the possibility of significant Chinese action, despite repeated warnings from the Indian ambassador in Peking and developing unease in the UN. The British chiefs of staff repeated their profound anxiety in October and this, in conjunction with the fears expressed by India, persuaded the British government to propose compromise, to be achieved through the establishment of a buffer zone [61, pp. 634–5]. The UNC, meanwhile, pressed on northwards. Progress was more rapid in the east than the west: by 19 October UNC troops advanced well beyond the port of Hungnam while in the west they were poised to enter the North Korean capital, Pyongyang. The latter was duly entered and 'liberated'. Thereafter further advances took place swiftly in the east and more American troops landed in the newly conquered territory on 26 October. Progress in the west was much slower. By 24 November, the greatest time of UNC occupation of the DPRK, UNC forces were on the Yalu in the east, near Hyesan-jin, and were approaching Chosan in the west. In the east, Chongjin, on the Soviet border, was arrived at by 24 November.

MacArthur's advance was too swift and reckless. He had divided his forces and failed to consolidate a defensible line in the course of which the British proposal, advanced earlier in November, for a buffer zone, could have been applied. The UNC was extremely vulnerable to a sudden Chinese attack [59, pp. 219–20].

Chinese intervention

Chinese forces crossed the Yalu on 16 October and moved into Korea. American and British intelligence reported the growing mobilisation in Manchuria and the Chinese involvement but the scale of the Chinese intervention was seriously underestimated. The first definite evidence of Chinese participation materialised towards the end of October. A defeat was inflicted on ROK troops on 28 October: it transpired that Chinese 'volunteers' were responsible. American troops were compelled to act in order to stiffen ROK resistance. Some Chinese were captured and it became obvious that China was involved directly, although the extent was unclear. Support for compromise to prevent escalation grew in the UN and was well-illustrated in proposals advanced by the British foreign secretary, Ernest Bevin. The British chiefs of staff, who had warned presciently of the perils since September, joined in exchanges with the cabinet. Sir John Slessor informed the cabinet that huge Chinese forces were assembled in Manchuria but intervention in Korea as yet appeared limited [61, p. 634]. American intelligence believed that around 35 000 Chinese troops were in Korea. An increase in numbers of Soviet aircraft had occurred: Slessor thought these were piloted mostly by Chinese or North Koreans. In fact Russian pilots were involved in significant numbers but they were under orders not to speak Russian while flying and to wear Chinese uniforms [60, p. 220]. Slessor told the cabinet that realities had to be faced: it was impossible to pursue further the aim of rolling back communism from Korea. A dispassionate assessment was required and the conflict in Korea should be placed in global perspective – 'Korea was of no strategic importance to the democratic Powers; and further operations there should now be conducted with a view to preventing any extension of the conflict and avoiding any lasting commitment in this area' [59, p. 208]. The chiefs of staff envisaged establishing a viable line of defence extending across the 'neck' of Korea from Chongju to Takchon, roughly along the 40th parallel. In this way a buffer zone could be created and this could lead to a ccase-fire.

Slessor's proposal was sensible and commended itself to the cabinet. However, allowance was not made for the volatility of opinion in the United States. It was not possible for many Americans to adopt a dispassionate approach when the United States was bearing the brunt of the fighting; in addition, the growth of hysteria over the Cold War rendered it extremely difficult for the Truman administration to act as suggested. The British chiefs of staff became increasingly critical of MacArthur and of the strategy he was pursuing. MacArthur angrily condemned attempts to persuade him to change his approach. It was only just over a decade since the British government had recommended the Munich agreement and this had failed abjectly [59, p. 208]: MacArthur rejected 'appeasement', as he interpreted it. Historical analogies should be used sparingly and with awareness of the dangers. Unfortunately, Munich became a cliché and MacArthur was contributing to its evolution. President Truman showed a more conciliatory attitude when he addressed a press conference on 16 November. There was no desire in the United States for war with China, according to Truman.

Bevin decided to act more firmly and told Dean Acheson that China must be convinced that the UN wanted to avert a clash with China. He instructed the British chargé d'affaires in Peking, John

Hutchison, to convey this view to the most senior Chinese official he could see. In addition, the Indian government would be informed, since India enjoyed better relations with China than many other members of the UN. In private Acheson had some sympathy for the British action but it was not feasible, politically, for the Truman administration to go as far as Bevin wished. Hutchison met a senior Chinese official, Chang Han-fu, on 22 November and emphasised the wisdom of agreeing upon a buffer zone: he stated that he was advancing the proposal personally, which was the appropriate diplomatic approach, given the delicacy of his mission [59, p. 209]. Hutchison defined the zone as a 'cushion' existing on the Korean side of the border: military forces would withdraw from it and DPRK authorities would be responsible for governing it.

Within the UN apprehension existed regarding Chinese intentions. This stimulated Bevin into renewed endeavours to convince the Truman administration of the merits of his proposal. In contrast to Hutchison's 'personal' suggestions in Peking, Bevin proposed that a buffer zone should be administered under the aegis of UNCURK. Time was fast running out. MacArthur was continuing the drive north, ignoring the Chinese intervention of a month before. Since the beginning of November, few signs of overt Chinese action had been discerned. The Chinese commander, P'eng Teh-huai, was biding his time and waiting for MacArthur to render UN forces more vulnerable to a Chinese onslaught. In mid-November MacArthur's head of intelligence, General Charles Willoughby, reported that Chinese troops in Korea might total 70 000, to which figure had to be added approximately 82 000 NKPA troops, following the reforming discussed earlier [29, part 1, p. 329, footnote]. General Walker's Eighth Army, advancing in the west, revealed a more cautious approach in November and modified the speed of advance. In the east General Almond's troops landed as part of a naval operation [29, p. 330]. Almond showed a desire to advance swiftly. Hyesanjin was reached on 21 November and ROK troops took Chongjin.

Chinese dispositions in the first half of November indicated an expectation that the most vital part of the Chinese military effort would be concentrated on the western prong of the offensive. The Chinese troops totalled approximately 300 000. UNC reconnaissance detected nothing to suggest that a massive Chinese intervention was about to occur. The jaws of the trap were soon to close with brutal impact. ROK forces encountered significant numbers of Chinese on 25 November, an ominous sign of Chinese attacks to come: the Chinese used a combination of loud drums, gongs and cymbals to inspire dread in their enemies and to give the advantage to the Chinese in the ensuing action. Early limited engagements were transformed swiftly into savage conflict along the front [29, pp. 330–2]. Once the magnitude of the situation struck the Eighth Army, a precipitate withdrawal followed. General Farrar-Hockley has provided an apposite concise assessment of the reasons for the Chinese success:

> The Chinese had succeeded in destabilising the army by exercising again the skills manifested in early November: mastery of concealment and thus surprise; cross country marching over mountain and hill tracks remote from the roads which the United Nations forces were reluctant to leave; persistent attack in flank and rear almost without regard to casualties. Most importantly, for the longer run of operations, they had established a moral ascendancy. [29, part 1, p. 335]

The effects on UNC morale were grave. The trauma was most marked for Americans. They had moved north fast, overtaking the more cautious British, on the confident assumption that the war was approaching its end and that they might be home for Christmas. Winter was closing in and this accentuated the enthusiasm for ending the war soon. Instead they encountered fresh armies in large numbers and it was clear not that the war was over but that it was changing into a far more dangerous and unpredictable struggle. The blow was severe for MacArthur, Walker and Almond; their strategy was overconfident, rash and had accepted too many risks. The more cautious and defensive strategy recommended by the British defence chiefs was far wiser. However, even the latter strategy might not have averted Chinese action. Mao Tse-tung believed that China must demonstrate that it could not be ignored in an area vital to its interests. This resulted from the trend of Mao's thinking during the 1940s and was extended by the knowledge of the CCP's triumph so speedily under his leadership because of its rapport with the peasant masses and because of nationalism. Chinese intervention was directed most obviously at the United States and the UN but it was also aimed at the Soviet Union and the DPRK. Mao's allies had to learn the same lesson as his opponents – China was a force to be reckoned with.

4

Confusion and Instability

The most dangerous stage of the Korean war occurred in the first two months following full-scale Chinese intervention. The Eighth Army pursued a lengthy retreat back down the Korean peninsula: this represented the longest, most sustained retreat in the history of the American army. Great uncertainty prevailed for some weeks over the response of the United States and the repercussions for the UN. It is a fascinating example of the confusion created by a sudden, catastrophic reversal in fortunes. A number of possibilities could be discerned. The scenario of the initial phase of the war could repeat itself and the anti-communist forces could be compelled to fall back to south-east Korea and might be driven from the peninsula. Whether or not this transpired, the United States might decide to take drastic action against China, which could lead to a full war, possibly involving atomic weapons. Alternatively, the war might be stabilised in relative terms so that neither side could achieve outright victory without risking a world war: the logic would then dictate the holding of negotiations pointing to the conclusion of an armistice. Dire as matters were, it was possible that a dialogue could be opened with China that could produce a wider agreement including a solution to the vexed problem of Chinese membership of the UN. The secretary-general of the UN, Trygve Lie, and his officials in New York were acutely aware of the threat to the future of the UN itself and the need to prevent overreaction from the United States. Most member states of the UN shared this anxiety. The UN became involved in a hectic round of activity in December 1950 and January 1951 which failed to engender the kind of solution hoped for. The situation improved for the UN, ultimately, for military rather than political reasons.

For President Truman developments came as a cruel blow. Rollback seemed to offer the opportunity of restoring the reputation and vigour of his administration but this enticing prospect turned out to be a mirage. Worse, the mirage showed signs of becoming a nightmare. Truman and his colleagues faced profound challenges representing the most dangerous situation to occur since the end of the Second World War. The Berlin blockade of 1948–9 was highly dangerous but actual armed conflict did not occur during the blockade. In Korea savage warfare had raged since June 1950 and was rapidly intensifying. Fortunately Truman was not a man to panic [43]. He was a leader of tenacity and stubbornness and had previously displayed determination to surmount criticism and censure: domestically this was illustrated in his arguments with the Republicans between 1946 and 1948, culminating in Truman's surprise victory in the 1948 presidential election. In the international sphere Truman took key decisions in the unfolding of the Cold War and he surmounted the perils of the Berlin blockade. Dean Acheson was an able, industrious, if arrogant, secretary of state. General George Marshall was back in the cabinet having replaced the erratic Louis Johnson in September: Marshall was in poor health but agreed to serve at the president's request. He possessed enormous experience and sagacity. The joint chiefs of staff, headed by General Omar Bradley, had been deferential to MacArthur in the past and bore responsibility for the ambiguity inherent in certain of the instructions sent to MacArthur. Bradley tended to be rather simplistic in some of his statements but wider expertise was available collectively.

Attlee's visit to meet Truman

The most obvious danger of escalation at the end of November concerned possible use of the atomic bomb (20; 65). Consideration of using atomic weapons was a theme of contingency planning throughout the war. At the beginning of the conflict, the secretary of the British chiefs of staff committee observed on 28 June that the Americans might opt to use the atomic bomb. He commented: 'The effects of such action would be world wide and might well be very damaging. Moreover it would probably provoke a global war [59, p. 235]. This referred to the readjustment in the balance of power which occurred in August 1949 when the Soviet Union successfully tested an atomic bomb [48, p. 220]. This resulted from the strenuous efforts of Soviet scientists and the dedication and skill revealed in their pursuance of the atomic project: they received important information from Stalin's spies in the West, but it was primarily a Soviet achievement. MacArthur favoured selective use of the atomic weapon in Korea and against Chinese cities. In December 1950 and January 1951 the prevailing opinion among the American military was that it was most likely to be necessary to withdraw from Korea and use alternative methods of military and economic warfare against China. The shock to American prestige and confidence was so great that the temptation to resort to the atomic option was powerful. Under a weaker or more extreme American president, it is quite likely that this option would have been implemented. Fortunately Truman possessed abundant common sense and courage, combined with a healthy scepticism of military men.

However, Truman did make a famous reference to considering all options in a press conference he addressed at the end of November. His response to a question was accurate in confirming that various possibilities were under review, but it stimulated much alarm within the UN and its members. This was illustrated graphically in Britain where many Labour MPs feared that the United States might decide to use the atomic bomb. Backbench MPs representing a broad spectrum of opinion urged the prime minister, Clement Attlee, to fly to Washington to meet Truman. Apprehension, too, was felt by cabinet ministers. Hugh Gaitskell, the chancellor of the exchequer and the most prominent right-wing member of the cabinet, told Attlee that he should go to Washington immediately [59, p. 215]. Anxiety over Korea, felt in Britain and western Europe, embraced both the atomic contingency and the associated problem that American resources and attention might be focused disproportionately on Asia, to the detriment of bolstering western Europe against the Soviet Union. Ernest Bevin's health was continuing to decline: he could assist in looking after matters in London but Attlee would have to travel to Washington. Truman was not enthusiastic to see Attlee but could not refuse. The two leaders duly met in the presence of their chief advisers, and a frank exchange of views ensued. The issues were delicate and the scope for differing assessments was appreciable. Attlee and Truman respected each other but were not close in personal terms. Both believed in speaking candidly and neither was noted for indulging in diplomatic verbiage. Attlee tended to be taciturn with a preference for expressing his views succinctly while Truman preferred blunt statements. One basic divergence related to the British wish for securing a general settlement of East Asian issues so that China's distinct grievances would be pursued in addition to the war in Korea. Therefore, the Truman administration would have to confront Chinese representation in the UN and the future of Taiwan. Attlee stated that world opinion must be taken into account: it was important that the United States did not adopt a narrow approach. Grave as the situation was, opportunities existed for obtaining an improved relationship with China. Attlee also warned that attention should not be diverted from pursuing recognised priorities. Europe was more important than Asia – 'The West is, after all, the vital part in our line against communism' [59, p. 216]. Attlee repeated the British view that it was feasible to separate China from the Soviet Union, provided that the correct strategy was followed. Truman and Acheson took a different line. Truman expressed this bluntly when he said that the Soviet Union controlled China: 'they are satellites of Russia and will be satellites so long as the present Peiping [Peking] regime is in power' [59, p. 216]. Truman was not sanguine and described the situation as 'very dark' [59, p. 216].

Acheson argued that Britain should be contributing more to the UN's obligations in Korea. The British wanted a substantial American commitment in developing NATO: the American people expected full support for American policy in Korea. Attlee criticised MacArthur for possessing excessive power. Marshall sought to defend him but Acheson's exasperation with MacArthur was evident in his comment as to whether anybody could control MacArthur. Truman and Attlee agreed that it was essential to stabilise the military situation in Korea and that Korea should be evacuated solely for *military* reasons (that is to say, not for political reasons linked with transferring the centre of conflict from Korea to China). Fundamental divergence over China was unavoidable. Acheson expressed some sympathy for the British preference for withdrawing recognition from the Kuomintang regime of Chiang Kai-shek but predictably added that the political temperature in the United States meant that no change was possible at this point. With reference to the atomic bomb, Truman appreciated the alarm voiced in Britain and among others in the UN: Britain would be consulted further unless the Soviet Union launched a sudden attack on the United States. Acheson felt Truman had gone too far in promising full consultation and qualified the position later in the exchanges.

The Truman–Attlee talks achieved a rather better understanding but did not represent a basic attainment of an agreed position. As the two leaders recognised, all would hinge ultimately on the military situation in Korea and whether this could be stabilised [21]. In the meantime the UN secretariat was involved in diplomatic exchanges with Chinese emissaries in an attempt to improve relations with Peking. Nehru, the Indian prime minister, worked zealously to promote negotiations. Mao Tse-tung and Chou En-lai were in a buoyant frame of mind in December and, while supporting exchanges with the UN in New York, were adamant that the PRC would not make major concessions. China wanted admission to the UN with the expulsion of the Kuomintang regime and a solution to the impasse over Taiwan which would accept that the latter should come under the authority of the PRC. An end to the Korean war could only be accomplished through agreement on the withdrawal of foreign troops and termination of American-inspired aggression in East Asia. The insuperable problem facing the UN cease-fire committee was that neither side was willing to make basic concessions. Acheson indicated at one point that the United States might be more flexible but he acted on the cynical assumption that China would not reciprocate, which would allow the Truman administration to revert to its unyielding approach over matters concerning China.

The retreat of UNC forces

The military position for the UNC was depressing with no sign of improvement. Having retired a considerable distance in the latter part of December, it was hoped that the Eighth Army could main-tain a position approximately along the 38th parallel. The Chinese forces advanced gradually and clashes in the vicinity of the 38th parallel involved the use of North Korean guerrillas. The Chinese required adequate supplies and General Peng Teh-huai was faced with ever-extending lines of communication. The commander of the Eighth Army, General Walton Walker, was killed in a road accident on 23 December. He was replaced by General Matthew B. Ridgway who brought a fresh approach and deep tenacity to bear. Ridgway believed that morale in UNC forces must be strengthened urgently and that to fall into accepting possible evacuation of Korea would be disastrous [29, part 1, p. 383]. It took him a little time to establish himself but his impact was then to be felt powerfully and positively. Amidst the severity of winter weather, bitter conflict resumed and raged as the year 1951 dawned. Neither side was equipped properly for the extremes in temperature and often lacked adequate clothing; some of the Chinese did not have boots. P'eng Teh-huai favoured stopping slightly north of the 38th parallel in late December for one to two months. Mao was keen to see his troops capture Seoul but recognised the exigencies as reported by P'eng. However, it was important for psychological reasons to cross the 38th parallel and, if possible, to take Seoul. The Chinese forces enjoyed success as the 'Third Phase Offensive' began on 31 December. UNC troops retired and Seoul was captured. MacArthur viewed the situation gloomily and regarded withdrawal from Korea as increasingly probable. He inclined to the opinion that all-out war with China would occur. In reality matters were not as bad as they seemed because Chinese lines of communication were stretched excessively and the Chinese troops lacked sufficient resources for an advance to the Pusan redoubt [29, part 2, p. 38]. In turn this assumed that UNC confidence could be restored, as Ridgway desired. Little sign of this could be discerned at the beginning of January 1951.

Alarm grew within UN member states and was illustrated clearly in British reactions. The British military adviser in Tokyo reported critically at the end of 1950 on the pessimism pervading MacArthur's headquarters and the emphasis placed on the size of the opposing Chinese armies, which could only have detrimental effects on morale. It looked as though MacArthur was accepting at least the inevitability of a retreat to the Pusan redoubt. This news provoked firm responses in London. Fears were expressed in the cabinet and Foreign Office and among the chiefs of staff that the understandings reached in the Truman–Attlee talks were to be vitiated. Commonwealth prime ministers were present in London early in January 1951 for one of their regular conferences and a mixture of anguish and criticism emerged. Nehru was most vocal in castigating American policy. Robert Menzies of Australia emphasised that the United States was carrying most of the burden in Korea and a strong United States was wholly essential to the global struggle to contain communism [61, pp. 632–9]. The chiefs of staff reckoned that enemy strength comprised approximately 350 000 Chinese troops and 170 000 North Korean troops. It is significant that the British estimate of Chinese strength was much lower than the American estimate. Large-scale Chinese reserves were in Manchuria, perhaps around 400 000, and could be moved rapidly into Korea. UNC military strength amounted to around 350 000; this included approximately 130 000 ROK men. Total UNC strength included seven American divisions, two British brigades, a Turkish brigade, some independent battalions provided by other UN states plus ten ROK divisions; certain of the latter could not be regarded as reliable. Chinese and North Korean air strength was limited and it was likely that the Soviet Union had dispatched Russian pilots to participate in the vicinity of the Manchurian border.

The British chiefs of staff argued that it was not in the interests of anyone for full-scale war against China to occur. Chinese cities could be eliminated through using the atomic bomb but China was largely a peasant society, accustomed to suffering, deprivation and war. It was not easy to see how China could be brought to admit defeat. The main beneficiary of a conflict between China and the UN would be the Soviet Union, not least because the West would be compelled to transfer resources from Europe to Asia. China would encourage revolutionary movements throughout South-East Asia. This could produce a ripple turning into a huge wave of dissent. The 'rice bowl of Asia' would be in communist hands with grave consequences for India, Ceylon, Malaya and Japan [59, p. 222]. Hong Kong might be taken. Some exaggeration could be seen in the arguments but in essence the chiefs of staff were correct to warn of the highly dangerous concomitants of a major war between the West and China. The Commonwealth leaders reiterated the importance of securing a comprehensive settlement of East Asian disputes. The familiar items of Chinese representation of the UN and the fate of Taiwan appeared again. The aim should be to obtain a cease–fire and then move on to discussion of outstanding issues involving China and Korea.

British representations in Washington

It was impossible to secure a clear statement from Washington on American policy: the Truman administration appeared traumatised. The British cabinet and chiefs of staff held that unless strong pressure was applied in Washington, a UNC military collapse could transpire, to be followed by war against China. Sir John Slessor observed sombrely, 'It appeared to him [Slessor] possible that General MacArthur now intended to withdraw from Korea and, having done so, to attack China by sea and air, making use of Chinese Nationalists to attack China on land' [59, pp. 232–4]. The cabinet decided to send Slessor to Washington for full exchanges with the American joint chiefs of staff. Slessor had to pursue certain vital questions, discussed by Attlee and Truman a month before. Slessor departed for Washington in the middle of January and was assisted in his deliberations by senior defence personnel from the British embassy. He spoke trenchantly of the anxiety and bewilderment in Britain and the Commonwealth. The situation could deteriorate quickly and lead to all-out war with China or to a third world war. The West was ready for neither eventuality. A widespread feeling existed in Britain that MacArthur was unduly motivated by political considerations and that the administration in Washington did not exercise enough authority in dealing with him. Slessor understood the dilemma facing the Truman administration and did not wish to indulge in futile recrimination. What was required was a clear definition of aims and agreement on genuine consultation to surmount past misunderstandings.

There was no shortage of combustible material in Slessor's analysis. The American response was in part conciliatory and in part critical. General Omar Bradley emphasised the basic aim of punishing aggression in Korea. North Korea had started the war and China chose to intervene. Unpalatable as it might be, the reality was that the UN and China were fighting each other in Korea. Europe was the priority and the Truman administration did not wish to see further resources dispatched to Asia. Bradley was pessimistic on the immediate predicament and deemed it impossible to establish a line currently [61, p. 641]. He anticipated withdrawal with an attempt to defend a limited area around Pusan. He confirmed Truman's commitment, made to Attlee in December, of remaining in Korea for as long as possible. Bradley did not think the Pusan redoubt could be held for long and withdrawal from Korea would then be unavoidable. He observed that relations between the United States and its allies in the UN were strained through a combination of military exigency and growing weariness of American public opinion with the UN itself: isolationism was reviving. The American defence chiefs wanted a resolution carried in the UN General Assembly condemning China as an aggressor and this would be followed by the application of an economic blockade. Dean Rusk, assistant secretary of state for far eastern matters, emphasised that China was threatening to expand with particular reference to Taiwan and Indo-China and perhaps Hong Kong. Rusk advocated a rigorous economic blockade of China.

Rusk and Bradley would have welcomed changes in British policy concerning diplomatic relations with Peking and Taiwan. Slessor and Sir Oliver Franks, the British ambassador, repeated that British policy would not change. While there was disappointment at the PRC's refusal to use existing diplomatic channels properly, no constructive purpose would be served by suspending or terminating diplomatic relations with China. The British were sceptical as to whether China did have ambitious expansionist aims in East and South-East Asia, as Rusk had argued. Slessor and Franks reiterated the value of establishing a solid line of defence so as to obviate the need for further retreat.

Slessor's visit revealed starkly the tensions between the UN and the United States and the dangers of allowing the situation to deteriorate. It was important that a prominent and able defence chief had spoken as Slessor did. Suspicion of certain Labour cabinet ministers existed in Washington and was felt by some within the Truman administration [59, p. 208]. Slessor could not be accused of harbouring pronounced socialist sympathies or of being less than wholehearted in his opposition to communism. UN states contributing to the UNC wanted clarity, consultation and stability instead of confusion, evasion and uncertainty. What was needed was rugged determination and common sense applied to the immediate military situation instead of debating how to wage direct war against China or how far Chinese expansion might be extended. Ironically these very qualities were in the process of being implemented by General Ridgway [79]. A gradual improvement in the UNC's position occurred from around 20 January 1951 and the principal credit belonged to Ridgway who, by forceful personal example, convinced his troops that the Chinese offensive must be blocked: defeat for the UNC must be avoided. Military developments will be considered further in the next chapter.

The UN and China

We shall turn now to the controversial topic of formal UN condemnation of China. The shock and bitterness resulting from China's actions since November 1950 led to determination to punish the PRC as firmly as was feasible short of full-scale conflict. Truman and Acheson wanted to utilise any means of castigating China and the best way of achieving this was to ensure that a resolution was carried in the UN General Assembly. This would place on record the revulsion felt within the UN, as the Truman administration saw it, and provide a basis for applying drastic economic sanctions. Vocal critics in the Republican party, such as Senators Robert A. Taft, Sr, William Knowland, Richard Nixon and Joseph McCarthy, deplored the alleged weakness, incompetence or treachery of the Democratic administration and urged tough action against the PRC [3; 78]. The right-wing Republicans were in full cry, zealous to undermine the administration further and to enhance their chance of securing the presidential nomination for a right-winger in 1952. There was considerable resentment at the lack of full support from the allies of the United States, particularly Britain. This reaction also applied to many Democrats including members of the administration. Dean Acheson often vented annoyance at what he deemed carping criticism from those who were not contributing as much as they could. In Acheson's case it was suspected that he sought to use pressure in return so as to prevent criticism from becoming louder. Truman and Acheson were in an invidious situation and they had to navigate as effectively as they could. The Labour government in Britain was regarded with some suspicion in the light of its domestic policy. Britain urged a substantially increased American commitment to Europe and the fostering of NATO but would not contribute more to a region in which the Cold War had become 'hot'. Britain's trading links with China via Hong Kong were seen as assisting the PRC's war effort. Acheson believed that the British protested excessively and were too concerned to protect their commercial interests in Hong Kong and with endeavouring to regalvanise trade with China, once the acrimony resulting from the Korean war abated. However, America did not wish to risk provoking a communist take-over of Hong Kong so that the British had some scope to manoeuvre in diplomatic arguments with Washington. Anglo-American disputes over Hong Kong and trade with China will be discussed further in later chapters.

American advocacy of a condemnatory resolution in the UN General Assembly coincided with a period of profound anxiety over American policy in China. Concern affected each political party in Britain and public opinion. The Labour party was most seriously affected because it included a number of MPs, trade unionists and rank-and-file activists who tended to be suspicious of policies pursued in Washington. The majority of the party was moderately pro–American but a vociferous minority existed. Debates in the Attlee cabinet late in January are revealing in that opposition to the proposed American resolution was stronger than might have been expected. The UN Cease-fire Committee was still attempting to secure a compromise but the efforts were doomed by the intransigence of both the United States and China. Mao Tse-tung derived encouragement from the visible splits within the UN and hoped these could be exploited. As Mao saw it, there was no need for China to make concessions when its troops were doing well and the UN was in disarray. Kim Il Sung wanted an unyielding policy applied, since he required time to rebuild the NKPA and to strengthen his dented authority in the DPRK. From Stalin's viewpoint, the position was positive: the United States and China were embroiled in circumstances which could only strengthen the power of the Soviet Union. With luck the rift within the capitalist side might widen to the benefit of communism and, to be more specific, the Soviet Union.

Attlee and Bevin warned Acheson that British support should not be taken for granted and that the United States should show adequate appreciation for the alarm felt in the UN. References by American officials to a possible extension of bombing were regrettable and dangerous. A telegram from Bevin, sent on 23 January 1951, warned that 'It must be brought home to the United States that it is not the rest of the world which is out of step with them but their own public opinion which is out on a limb by itself' [59, p. 228]. Within the cabinet Aneurin Bevan, James Griffiths, Hugh Dalton and Chuter Ede were to the fore in criticising the draft terms of the American resolution for the UN. Of this group only Bevan could be described as unequivocally on the left-wing of the party. Kenneth Younger, the minister of state in the Foreign Office, was irritated at the overbearing American approach and held that it would be salutary in the longer perspective for Britain to be prepared to vote against the American proposal in the General Assembly. This line was opposed vehemently by the most prominent pro-American member of the cabinet, Hugh Gaitskell. As chancellor of the exchequer, he was only too conscious of the necessity for American support for the fragile British economy. The cabinet agreed on 25 January that Britain would contemplate voting against the American resolution unless the terms were rendered more acceptable. Acheson decided to adopt limited concessions, since it would be too embarrassing if the two countries diverged markedly at a delicate time. Attlee agreed with Gaitskell that a row with Washington should be averted; after additional exchanges the cabinet agreed to support the resolution [59, p. 228–9]. The General Assembly carried the resolution on 1 February with Britain voting in favour.

This pattern of exchange was not untypical in the course of the Korean war. American will prevailed but the more militant, truculent manifestations in American policy could be modified to persuade America's allies to keep in line. Plenty of difficulties remained but the most traumatic phase of the Korean conflict for the UN drew to a close at the beginning of February 1951. The extremely fluid situation created by China's actions in November 1950 began to stabilise as the military fortunes of the UNC started slowly to improve. It was less likely that the UN would be compelled to evacuate Korea. The great Chinese offensive was slowing as the magnitude of the operations hit home in the depth of winter. The Eighth Army, firmly committed to remaining in Korea, was the most encouraging feature and counterbalanced the alarm caused by General MacArthur's pronouncements.

5

The Departure of MacArthur

Gradually the Korean war moved into a more encouraging phase for the UNC between February and May 1951. A new spirit of resilience was shown by the UNC and China failed in its endeavour to smash UNC confidence. On the other hand, the UNC was embroiled in deep controversy over the role of its commander-in-chief, MacArthur, and this culminated in the latter's dismissal in April. General Matthew B. Ridgway appeared at the right time for the challenges facing him. He was able, courageous, dedicated, without the airs and graces that rendered other generals less attractive. He had no political aspirations. Ridgway perceived his task as one of instilling confidence and vigour into his assorted troops. General Farrar-Hockley captures the character of Ridgway well in his official history of the British military role in Korea. Ridgway travelled extensively to meet UNC forces. Towards the end of January 1951 he met a group of British artillerymen, tank crews and others, south of Suwon, on a cold, crisp morning. He climbed out of his jeep and said: 'I want you all to know that I am not going to fight for a particular piece of Korean real estate. If they attack us before we are ready, we shall roll along with the punches. But then we shall attack them when they are extended. They may have the numbers but we have the firepower' [29, part 2, p. 31]. Ridgway soon made it clear that he expected his orders to fight effectively to be obeyed and that he would act appropriately against officers disregarding such orders.

On 11 February P'eng Teh-huai launched the 'Fourth Phase-Offensive' [76]. P'eng was under pressure from Mao to occupy the area north of the line from Taejon to Andong. The operation was premature in that P'eng's men were handicapped by injury and exhaustion, apart from the interference with supply lines caused by UNC air attacks. Savage fighting ensued in the east and west, frequently in very low temperatures. British troops were prominent in February and March, involving notably the Royal Ulster Rifles, the Glosters and the Northumberland Fusiliers. The UNC was making significant progress. By 21 February it was clear that a significant change for the better had been effected in consequence of the new tough leadership provided by Ridgway. Chinese and North Korean attempts to break through had been frustrated. UNC forces were again moving north and the familiar issue of crossing the 38th parallel loomed once more. Within the Truman administration and in the UN it was appreciated that the importance of driving back the enemy was not to reproduce the scenario of October 1950,

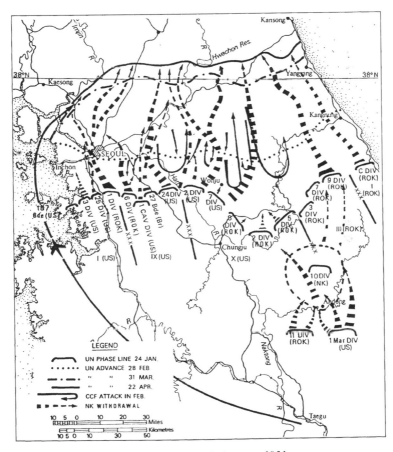

Map 5   *The campaign, November 1950–January 1951*

which was in any case impossible, but to establish sufficient strength to emphasise that the UNC would stand firm. The implication was that a cease-fire would ensue and this would lead to a termination of the war which would be linked to a broader settlement of disputes involving China. The British chiefs of staff adhered to their recommendation of caution: after liberating Seoul for the second time, UNC forces should stop at the 38th parallel. What was required in order to commence cease-fire talks was an awareness and acceptance by the communist states that a military victory was impossible and that the Korean war should be brought to an end. However, at this stage the communist states did not see matters in this light. Mao Tse-tung believed that China could still secure a vital breakthrough and instructed P'eng to prepare for another offensive [29, part 2, p. 38]. Kim Il Sung was desperate to place the DPRK in as strong a position as possible and was opposed to compromise. Stalin was content to await the outcome of Chinese military action. Therefore, the United States and the UNC were ahead of their enemies in considering negotiations. The United States held that rigorous economic measures against China would improve coordination among UN states participating in Korea and would eventually convince the PRC, in conjunction with a military stalemate, to negotiate. Economic action against China was a most contentious area to which we must now turn.

Economic sanctions

From the American viewpoint, application of economic measures was essentially straightforward to contemplate. Diplomatic relations did not exist between Washington and Peking. The United States unenthusiastically continued to recognise the Kuomintang administration of Chiang Kai-shek in Taiwan, although the authority of the latter was limited to islands off the China coast and to a few scattered border areas where resistance continued with help from American agencies. There was no direct trade between the United States and China. Trade did take place between Japan and mainland China. The relevant point here is that the United States was primarily responsible for the administration of Japan under the allied occupation. When Britain came to be criticised more strongly by some Americans, including MacArthur, for trading with the enemy, the British Foreign Office investigated the extent of trade between Japan and mainland China in 1950 and in the first three months of 1951. Some interesting information on commercial links between Japan and China appeared in the American press. The outcome was that Japanese exports to China in 1950 were estimated to total US$16 million and most of these comprised iron and steel manufactured goods. The American authorities in Tokyo approved Japanese exports consisting of cotton fabrics, bicycles, woven silk, sewing machines, cotton yarn, filament and paper. Following China's entry into the Korean war, exports of raw materials and semi-processed goods were stopped. In the first three months of 1951 Japanese exports to China increased each month from US$493 000 in January, to $827 000 in February, to US$1 063 000 in March [59, p. 131]. The United States and MacArthur condoned trade with China. Of course, for obvious geographical reasons commerce between Japan and China was bound to occur and Yoshida Shigeru, Japanese prime minister from 1948 to 1954, said on several occasions that, notwithstanding his hostility to communism, he looked forward to expanding trade with China [24, pp. 394–5; 8, pp. 44–5]. Even MacArthur, despite his hatred of 'Red China', accepted before June 1950 that trade would develop in future.

The British government faced various dilemmas in relation to trade with China [30; 110; 85]. The Chinese government detested imperialism of any kind. Foreign businessmen reminded Chinese leaders of past humiliation inflicted on China, frequently in the name of trade and with large profits being made from exploitation of the toiling masses of Chinese workers and peasants. Mao and his senior colleagues regarded British recognition of the PRC cynically as a step taken reluctantly by a government under the thumb of the United States in most respects: the British wished to defend their interests in Hong Kong and hoped to revive trade with China. Hong Kong was particularly difficult. The crown colony was highly vulnerable in the event of a major dispute developing between Britain and China. Mao wanted to end foreign imperialism but had to accept that the return of Hong Kong would most likely have to be postponed until 1997. Chinese leaders soon realised that there were advantages in tolerating the status quo in Hong Kong [14, pp. 96–122]. China could obtain goods required and could establish a useful base for intelligence purposes through the New China News Agency. Thereby a watch could be kept on British activities, American visitors, the local agents of the Kuomintang and other relevant aspects. Indeed, Hong Kong quickly became a humming centre of rival intelligence agencies from different countries (and sometimes the same country), all spying on each other. Hong Kong was administered by a governor appointed by the Colonial Office: the current incumbent was Sir Alexander Grantham. Understandably, the Colonial Office developed a particular sense of responsibility towards Hong Kong, which involved mastering the realities of running the colony and disapproving of outside pressure which could complicate the benign autocracy of British rule (more democratic methods of administering Hong Kong were eschewed as too dangerous and undesirable). The governor was not inclined to cooperate too enthusiastically with American zeal for curbing commerce. The Foreign Office was more aware, before and after the passage of the resolution approved in the UN General Assembly on 1 February, of the necessity for handling such matters skilfully.

Some friction occurred within the British bureaucracy. The United States was adamant that strategic materials must be denied to China: concern was voiced particularly over rubber, drugs, metals, trucks, steel plates and raw materials, including cotton. The State Department felt more could and should be done by the British authorities in Hong Kong. The feeling was expressed much more vehemently in Congress and in much of the American press [59, pp. 129–33]. The British were depicted as grumbling about American policy in Korea while contributing only a limited amount to the fighting; furthermore they continued to trade with a state whose troops were killing Americans (and some British) in Korea. British officials met at the beginning of March 1951 and identified strategic items which should be placed on a list of banned goods. The items included machine tools, vehicles, electronic equipment, non-ferrous metals and ferro-alloys. American critics focused notably on rubber exports. Britain permitted average rubber exports to China of 13 000 tonnes per month in the period from January to March 1951. Thereafter the quota was cut to 2500 tonnes a month. The Foreign Office was defensive over rubber exports and favoured a tougher approach. The accumulating pressures from the United States for full compliance, with sanctions imposed under UN authority, forced Britain to tighten policy in May and June 1951. Britain implemented full export licence control and embargo to apply in colonies and dependent territories in an endeavour to placate the Americans. A more thorough licensing policy would be enforced in Hong Kong. An additional resolution was carried in the

UN General Assembly on 18 May 1951 and British officials gave assurances to Washington that Britain would cooperate whole-heartedly. Members of the Truman administration were largely placated, but some Republican politicians extended their criticism of a weak or duplicitous ally.

The dismissal of MacArthur

The principal development in March and April 1951 concerned the arguments over the role of General MacArthur which reached its climax when President Truman dismissed MacArthur from all offices held under the American government and the UN. In the early part of the war disagreements between MacArthur and Truman were limited, the most conspicuous divergence concerning MacArthur's visit to Taiwan (31 July to 1 August) and his blunt message to the Veterans of Foreign Wars in August. Both men wanted to see North Korea defeated swiftly and both relished the prospect of rollback. MacArthur was permitted considerable freedom for manoeuvre: undoubtedly he possessed more independence than would have obtained had a general of less eminence held the post he occupied. But the roots of more fundamental divergence were present from the start. MacArthur was autocratic, elderly, not inclined to listen to opinions contrary to his own, and attracted by the prospect that he could yet secure the most powerful office open to a citizen of the United States [49; 81]. For MacArthur all was transformed by developments in the last week of November 1950. The great victorious commander was replaced by a commander who had gravely underestimated the enemy and suffered the consequences. MacArthur became more difficult to deal with, more remote and more petulant. Ridgway's success in reviving morale and confidence in the Eighth Army undermined MacArthur's standing. the joint chiefs of staff began to communicate directly with Ridgway and MacArthur's power declined. Criticism of MacArthur mounted in Britain and in the UN from the end of November 1950 onwards. Despite his past achievements in the Pacific war and in the initial stages of the Korean conflict, there was no faith whatever in his capacity to contribute constructively to a solution in Korea. British representatives aimed, through repre-sentations in Washington, to diminish his power and preferably to see him replaced by a more congenial commander – Ridgway was the obvious choice [61, pp. 641–3]. Foreign criticism was a double-edged weapon: pressure on the Truman administration intensified but this could render it more difficult to curb the general, since his supporters – and possibly the American public – would resent outside censure. The only person who could merge all aspects and achieve the circumstances appropriate to his removal was paradoxically MacArthur himself.

In the six weeks preceding his removal, MacArthur followed a course of action that produced such circumstances. He disapproved of the administration's wish to negotiate with China and the DPRK to end the war. He viewed China as a bigger threat than the Soviet Union and held that confrontation and conflict were inevitable. In March he deliberately undermined Truman's wish to begin exchanges with China through making a public statement of his own in which he placed the emphasis on military victory, adding that he was prepared to meet the Chinese commander-in-chief if this would assist in concluding the war [49, pp. 585–7]. This statement achieved the aim of torpedoing any prospect of starting talks at this juncture. MacArthur compounded his defiance in correspondence with the Republican minority leader in the House of Representatives, Joseph W. Martin, and in a press interview given to a British general [49, pp. 589–90]. MacArthur had long maintained contacts with sympathetic Republicans in Congress, extending back to the Pacific campaigns: Martin was a congenial and important Republican. The latest correspondence was released by Joe Martin on 5 April 1951: MacArthur frankly attacked the policy of the administration he served for weakness in dealing with communism and for putting excessive stress on Europe, to the detriment of Asia. Truman was deeply affronted and the long-simmering crisis moved into an explosive phase. Truman had already received growing foreign criticism of MacArthur for acting in too cavalier a manner, incompatible with his responsibilities.

In Britain condemnation of the general increased. Herbert Morrison had succeeded the dying Ernest Bevin as foreign secretary in March 1951. Morrison knew little of foreign policy but a great deal about the inner workings of the Labour party. As 'boss' of the London Labour party, Morrison was well-aware of disapproval of MacArthur growing rapidly in the party. He wanted to make an early impact in the Foreign Office, since he wished to advance his career so that he could succeed Attlee as leader and prime minister. Morrison was less inhibited than Bevin had been in expressing British criticisms more vigorously in Washington [59, p. 231]. He urged that the president should issue a statement clarifying objectives. On 5 April the text of an interview between MacArthur and the military correspondent of the *Daily Telegraph* newspaper, Lieutenant-General H. G. Martin, was published. MacArthur blamed politicians for the mess in Korea. Aims had not been defined adequately; the debate over crossing the 38th parallel resulted from the ineptitude of politicians. He stated that he had been handicapped by political leaders reluctant to face realities: China could be defeated quite easily if the politicians would 'take the wraps off' [61, p. 647]. The Chinese economy was weak and vulnerable. A comprehensive blockade of China plus the destruction of the Chinese railway system would undermine the Chinese war effort seriously. The contribution of British troops was applauded. MacArthur brushed aside possible intervention in Korea by the Soviet Union but warned that a new Chinese offensive would be launched in May. Morrison decided that he must make a parliamentary statement along the lines of deprecating MacArthur's statements, confirming the UN's commitment to democratic reunification of Korea, opposing a widening of the conflict and recommending careful adhesion to the UN's role in acting in Korea.

Truman probably decided to dismiss MacArthur in March but it was essential to consult senior members of his administration and the joint chiefs of staff [98]. Truman faced one of the most delicate challenges of his presidency, involving a leader whose poll ratings were falling removing a distinguished general perceived as a hero by many Americans. However, Truman was not one to follow opinion polls: he had famously proved the pollsters to be wrong in November 1948 when he defeated Governor Dewey to remain in the White House. Truman consulted Dean Acheson, General George Marshall, Averell Harriman, the joint chiefs plus Vice-President Alben Berkeley. The position was reviewed fully and Marshall perused past correspondence with MacArthur. This task incensed the loyal Marshall, for the full extent of MacArthur's insubordination and defiance was revealed. All consulted were unanimous that MacArthur must depart. It was intended that Army Secretary Frank Pace, who was visiting Japan, should notify MacArthur personally. Fears of press leaks led to a premature press announcement so that MacArthur was informed by his wife who had heard the news on the radio. His reaction was that at last they would be going home (he had not visited the United States since 1938) [49, p. 600].

The dismissal was welcomed in Britain and the UN. It bequeathed considerable problems of uncertain resolution. How would Congress and the American people react? What would emerge from investigations of the causes of MacArthur's dismissal? Could there be a backlash of support for MacArthur with a consequent encouragement of isolationist or 'Asia-first' policies? The immediate reaction among the public was to view MacArthur through strongly rose-tinted spectacles. He received generous, even ecstatic welcomes in American cities on his return. It was highly emotional and criticism of Truman increased. Many Republicans lavished extravagant praise on MacArthur and seized another opportunity to castigate the administration. Demands for a thorough inquiry into the reasons for his dismissal led to the convening of joint Senate hearings by the Foreign Relations and Armed Services sub-committees chaired by Richard Russell (Democrat, Georgia). The inquiry began in May in a highly charged atmosphere. The first witness was MacArthur himself. The general was in part impressive and in part disappointing. The charisma was as potent as ever. He did not regard the Soviet Union as constituting a major threat in East Asia and he did not want American troops to fight in mainland China. The British colony in Hong Kong assisted China with trade and British defence personnel had not communicated with MacArthur to state anxiety over crossing the 38th parallel. MacArthur made clear his total condemnation of British policy concerning China – 'Now I believe sincerely that the fundamental interest of the British is involved in this question of the Western Pacific and I believe most sincerely that they are cutting their own throats in following the plans they have of such complete support of the giving of Formosa into the hands of a potential Red enemy' [61, p. 650]. In the main senators treated MacArthur deferentially. The sharpest questioning came from two Democrats and a maverick Republican – J. William Fulbright (Democrat, Arkansas), Brien McMahon (Democrat, Connecticut) and Wayne Morse (Republican, Oregon). At times MacArthur was too expansive and on other occasions too evasive. His memory was fallible occasionally. Nothing sensational came out of his testimony and few opinions changed as a result.

A number of other witnesses appeared but interest in the hearings gradually diminished. The star witness had come and gone and the loquacious contributions of certain senators accelerated waning public enthusiasm. By the end it was clear that Truman had succeeded in demonstrating that he had acted correctly in upholding the dignity and constitutional authority of his office. Americans possess deep respect for the office of president and for the constitution and the majority came to feel, sadly, that a great general had overstepped the mark and had to be curbed. In this respect the outcome was reassuring for Britain and other members of the UN. MacArthur did not forgive criticism from Britain and the UN, as was made clear in speeches he delivered subsequently. However, MacArthur lacked political skills and was unlikely to gain the Republican nomination in 1952. His political significance lay in the use of his dismissal by fellow right-wing Republicans as a rallying-point for renewed attacks on Truman and Acheson.

While members of the UN could celebrate the departure of MacArthur, they could not assume that problems in the relationship between the United States and the UN would diminish, let alone disappear. Dean Acheson wanted to seize the opportunity to pursue a more resolute approach and to persuade the allies of the United States to accept a stiffening in American policy towards China. This is illustrated in a telegram sent from the State Department to the embassy in London on 17 April:

> Stated another way now is time for us to 'cash in' on new situation arising because of removal of MacArthur from scene. In this connection most important for Britain to understand that this does not mean change in our position vis-à-vis Chinese Commies which if changed in any way will be in direction of increased firmness. [61, p. 649]

Ridgway's contribution

We shall now revert to considering the course of the military campaigns. In March Ridgway concentrated on a gradual advance without being too ambitious: his aim was to weaken the Chinese capacity for launching a new offensive. By the end of March enemy casualties numbered approximately 30 000 with around 4000 captured; the definite tally of enemy killed was 7409 at the end of March [29, part 2, p. 76, note 1]. The River Han was crossed successfully in March on both sides of Seoul and analogous advances were made in the east. But the Chinese armies retained their capacity to launch a further offensive. In the second half of March Ridgway directed the advance beyond Seoul and Ch'unch'on, hoping to gain the initiative in dealing with the North Korean I corps. He was frustrated by North Korean withdrawal. Ridgway now worked to establish a defensive line which was termed 'Kansas'. This would stabilise the position approximately along the 38th parallel. Ridgway urged improved efficiency upon his corp commanders, since he was dissatisfied with recent operations. The quality of staff work must be strengthened. Following MacArthur's dismissal, Truman appointed Ridgway to the posts held previously by MacArthur. General James Van Fleet succeeded Ridgway. The new head of UNC was viewed very favourably and he inspired trust, which could not have been said of his predecessor.

The Chinese offensive

Chinese preparations for the next offensive were fulfilled in April. P'eng Teh-huai emphasised to senior officers that meticulous care must be taken to maximise use of transport efficiently: this included utilising captured American vehicles. Approximately 500 000 men were available. P'eng aimed to attack by night whenever possible, using the terror tactics which the Chinese forces had deployed so effectively in previous campaigns. P'eng envisaged eliminating three American divisions, three British and Turkish brigades and two ROK divisions. All was ready for the clash on the Imjin river. The British troops, including the Northumberland Fusiliers and the Glosters, were very soon in the thick of savage fighting. The first minor clash occurred on 21 April when a small reconnaissance group was repulsed. On 22 April the Chinese advanced in earnest. Van Fleet gave orders that Line Kansas must be held if possible; areas should be defended by night with the aim of deploying potent fire by day subsequently. Van Fleet modified Ridgway's strategy in the sense of rendering it less flexible with emphasis more on tough resistance with implicit acceptance of higher casualties. As General Farrar-Hockley has observed, Van Fleet was intent on preserving recent improvement in morale, effected by Ridgway, and he did not want this undermined by early withdrawal [29, part 2, p. 124]. On 25 April it became clear that the Glosters were surrounded and a relief operation was cancelled. The Glosters were left with the challenge of breaking out. Chinese troops assailed the defensive line and fighting at short range developed. The Glosters fought with great courage and some succeeded in breaking out but UNC casualties were high, amounting to 1091 in three days; 622 officers and men were killed. Errors were made by senior American and British officers: the Glosters should not have been left in such a dangerously exposed predicament.

Ridgway conveyed his concern to Van Fleet who replied that, despite heavy losses, it was salutary that the Glosters had fought so bravely because it facilitated the evacuation of other troops including British – 'I feel that this Battalion was not lost in vain – that this is one of those great occasions in combat which call for a determined stand and the loss of 622 officers and men saved many times that number' [29, part 2, p. 135]. The Glosters had indeed played a vital role in delaying the advance of the 64th and 65th Chinese armies. The failure to secure a rapid breakthrough compelled P'eng Teh-huai to pause and reorganise. Van Fleet believed he could hold Seoul, although the Chinese were threatening to enter the city. American intelligence indicated that P'eng had large reserves, possibly around 300 000. P'eng aimed to eliminate the ROK-held sector which extended in the vicinity of the Taebaek mountains.

In the second half of May P'eng recognised reluctantly that his offensive had failed. The key factor was not the advance of UNC troops but rather the extent of Chinese casualties and losses of equipment. P'eng was proud of the losses suffered by the UNC, particularly with the so-called 'puppet' [ROK] losses. However, insufficient transport, food and ammunition, coupled with the appearance of American reinforcements, meant that 'it is becoming increasingly difficult for us to extend our offensive, and thus the Fifth Campaign is about to come to an end for the time being' [29, part 2, p. 157]. P'eng implemented a strategic retreat with the purpose of awaiting more fortuitous circumstances. The end of the offensive marked a termination of the frantic, bloody fighting occurring amidst the repeated tergiversations of the first eleven months of the Korean conflict. It was likely that the Soviet Union and China would now reach the conclusion arrived at three months before by the United States, Britain and other members of the UN. It was impossible to achieve a military victory and thoughts turned towards an armistice agreement.

6
The Start of
Armistice Talks

In the midst of the final Chinese offensive the American and British governments discussed the issue of possible retaliation in the event of China using bases in its own territory in order to attack the UNC. This was a delicate matter and had arisen on a number of occasions earlier in the war when American planes deliberately or accidentally attacked targets on Chinese or Russian territory. However, such attacks had not been in accordance with official policy and MacArthur and the air commander, Stratemeyer, issued a rebuke when explicit orders were disregarded [59, p. 201]. After the start of the new Chinese offensive late in April 1951, Acheson informed Herbert Morrison that retaliation should be applied if the Chinese used their own bases for aggressive purposes. The subject was controversial and conceivably dangerous, given the American enthusiasm for implementing rigorous economic sanctions against China. The Attlee cabinet agreed that retaliation against bases in Manchuria could be enforced if the situation justified it but there must be prior consultation. It was not a decision for which the Labour government wished to receive publicity, given the opinions held by left-wing MPs and party activists. In 1952 Winston Churchill, by then prime minister, announced the existence of the secret agreement in the House of Commons, to the ire of some Labour MPs and the embarrassment of former cabinet ministers [59, p. 252]. The failure of the Chinese offensive in May and a steady improvement in the position of the UNC obviated the need for retaliation, but the question arose again in the summer of 1952, following UNC bombing of dams in North Korea. The success enjoyed by the UNC in May 1951 led Ridgway to speculate that the war might be moving into a new stage: it was premature to conclude that a cease-fire might occur and much would depend on the policy of the Soviet Union. The Chinese had suffered considerable losses and their operations were hampered by unduly extended lines of communication, inadequate equipment and insufficient air strength.

Ridgway was correct in identifying the reaction of the Soviet Union as the vital consideration. Kim Il Sung was keen to maintain military activity, fearing that too many concessions could be made once negotiations began. Mao Tse-tung was disappointed with the outcome of the latest offensive but believed that there was no urgency in negotiating to achieve a cease-fire. Stalin followed a careful, adroit policy of what might be called 'active indirect intervention', since the shattering of the assumptions upon which he had based his original approval for a North Korean offensive in June 1950. Soviet defence personnel had been involved actively in advising Kim Il Sung's officers before and at the outset of the war. Soviet help in the air was crucial in supporting the Chinese and NKPA military campaigns [112, pp. 67–72]. Soviet planes and equipment played a major part in sustaining operations. But Stalin would not advance beyond this significant indirect role, even when Soviet territory was bombed, whether deliberately or not, on a few occasions. The Soviet Union was not prepared for escalation into a third world war. Stalin was not optimistic on the future and thought another world war was probable around the mid-1950s but he did not desire a world conflict in 1951 [48, p. 253]. Soviet aims had, in any case, been fulfilled partially in Korea, notably through the bitter hostility engendered between the United States and China. As Stalin rightly deduced, the Korean conflict ended any prospect of Sino-American *rapprochement* for the foreseeable future. In addition, while Kim Il Sung had failed in his bold attempt to unify Korea, the DPRK survived and it was obvious, in May 1951, that the UNC would be incapable of liquidating the DPRK. Indeed, American enthusiasm for rollback had diminished since November 1950 except in the rhetoric of right-wing American politicians.

Stalin supports armistice talks

Therefore Stalin decided that his policy should change. Since the support of the Soviet Union was so essential, the PRC and the DPRK acquiesced in diplomatic action approved by Stalin. The American State Department contemplated the situation in April and May and decided to set in motion its own diplomatic endeavours to secure a cease-fire in Korea. The chosen American agent was George Kennan, the original architect of the policy of containing the Soviet Union. Kennan had developed into a more independent figure within the State Department in the late 1940s and became too much of a maverick for the prevailing ethos in the State Department. Kennan did not enjoy the same power under Acheson that he had done under Acheson's predecessor, Marshall, and Kennan decided in 1950 to leave the public service. Before departing at the end of August 1950 he drafted perceptive criticism of American policy in Korea criticising the failure to identify fundamental aims clearly enough. Why then was he used as a key intermediary in May–June 1951? Primarily because Kennan was a great authority on Soviet foreign policy and because he possessed the requisite skills for undertaking highly delicate discussions while not being employed by the American government [91, pp. 204–9]. Kennan began a series of meetings with Jacob Malik, the Soviet delegate to the UN in New York. He knew Malik reasonably well and it was feasible to exchange opinions with Malik on possible ways of achieving progress. In the initial meeting Malik was somewhat restrained and emphasised problems in relations between the United States and the PRC. Kennan saw Malik again early in June when the latter confirmed that the Soviet Union wished to see an end to fighting in Korea. The green light could be discerned even if amber prevailed temporarily.

The change in Soviet policy became public on 23 June when Malik delivered a radio address in New York in a series of talks arranged by the UN. Predictably and unavoidably Malik uttered well-worn sentiments on the negative features of American foreign policy since 1945, but Malik then spoke of the Soviet desire for an improved relationship between the communist world and the West. The Soviet Union hoped that a cease-fire in Korea could be agreed. The reaction of the Truman administration was that the United States would respond positively, provided that the opposing states were genuine in their desire to terminate the fighting in Korea. Following this initial statement from the State Department, Truman spoke along similar lines when fulfilling an engagement in Tennessee on 25 June [59, p. 234]. These developments were welcomed in the UN. In Britain Morrison told the cabinet that the trend was encouraging, although due caution should be exercised until proof of Soviet professed aims materialised. One person who did not enthuse was Syngman Rhee: no doubt Kim Il Sung felt similarly. Rhee interpreted any indications of compromise as signifying weakness and possible betrayal, but he could only observe matters with a malign eye.

Thus, the Korean war changed, in June to July 1951, from a conflict of astonishing tergiversations, in which first one side and then the other launched vigorous, bloody campaigns, to a conflict in which military and air activity continued at a reduced, but sometimes ferocious level, while talks to obtain a cease-fire continued, originally at Kaesong and then at Panmunjom. The general feeling in the UN and, more broadly, in the West in July 1951 was that a cease-fire agreement would emerge after some months of possibly acrimonious exchange. Few anticipated that the talks at Panmunjom would drag on interminably until, at last, an agreement was signed, two years later, in July 1953. The challenges to both sides were very considerable, as will be seen, but neither approached the task of negotiating a cease-fire with sufficient care or expertise. Kennan and Malik were well-qualified for the preliminary exchanges but they were not responsible for the next stage. When the talks began in Kaesong and then transferred to Panmunjom, the military dominated discussions on both sides [33; 5]. Chinese and North Korean military delegates sat opposite American and South Korean delegates; of course, the Soviet Union was not participating and the same applied to Britain, although British forces were fighting in Korea. It was understandable that the military controlled the actual talks but it was unfortunate that diplomatic skills were not deployed in addition to the military. Each side regarded the other with contempt; each was proud of what had been accomplished militarily; each was conscious of its losses; each believed fervently that capitalism was superior to communism and vice versa; each saw merit in making tedious propaganda statements [51]. However, the acrimony was an extension of the basic suspicion that prevailed. Both sides knew that military victory was impossible but both feared that premature or unwise concessions could be made and developments must be scrutinised with great care. In short, there was a definite wish in the United States, UN, China and the Soviet Union to see the war ended, but none saw this as urgent and all felt that, given time, their opponents might weary first and make more concessions to them.

The American and British governments looked broadly at the range of issues in East Asia in July and August. The State Department was preoccupied with the fast-approaching conference in San Francisco, convened for the purpose of approving the Japanese peace treaty [107]. The Soviet Union would be attending but neither of the rival Chinese regimes would be present. The peace treaty was a cornerstone of American policy in Asia and was intended simultaneously to weld Japan into the western defence structure in Asia–Pacific and to guard against a possible revival of Japanese militarism [8; 31, pp. 241–316; 59, pp. 28–81]. American apprehension that the Soviet Union might cause trouble in San Francisco was not borne out: Gromyko, the Soviet foreign minister, criticised American policy in rebuilding Japan but made no serious endeavour to derail the conference. Looking beyond the signing of an armistice in Korea, it was important to start assessing the nature of a more ambitious settlement involving various outstanding problems in eastern Asia. One avenue would be for the UN General Assembly to establish a small group, perhaps comprising up to five representatives of states participating in the fighting in Korea, to negotiate with the communist states.

Trygve Lie, the UN secretary–general, proposed the appointment of one UN representative to act as a mediator and the State Department was willing to consider this further but was not in favour of a British suggestion for a five-power conference: the reason for the latter was that it could undermine American control. On wider matters involving South-East Asia or such problems as concerned Hong Kong or Tibet, a broader consultative conference could be assembled: this would bring together all countries with interests in the region. The British response was that the UN must be involved adequately and that the General Assembly should agree a resolution calling for consultation between appropriate govern-ments regarding a solution to the future of Korea. The ROK and the DPRK should participate and a UN mediator could assist. Britain favoured involving a small number of powers: the Soviet Union should be consulted once agreement had been reached by the United States and Britain concerning the next step. The State Department concurred that immediately after the signing of a cease-fire, political discussions should be restricted to Korea and that these should involve China and the DPRK. It was unlikely that the communist states would accept a UN mediator [59, pp. 240–2].

The start of armistice talks

The truce talks opened in Kaesong in July. Ridgway erred in agree-ing to the venue: Kaesong was situated within the DPRK and the atmosphere was too intimidating. The talks were then transferred to Panmunjom where each side could draw solace from having achieved an equal measure of background intimidation. On behalf of the UNC the talks were headed by Admiral C. Turner Joy: later, in 1952, he was succeeded by General William Harrison. The British government felt that the American approach lacked sufficient consistency and cohesion. At times American negotiators were too rigid and on other occasions appeared insufficiently careful. The danger was that the talks might fail if the United States was unduly tough or the position of the UNC could be weakened through American carelessness. Progress was made in agreeing that the question of foreign troops leaving Korea should be deferred, therefore facilitating pursuance of more urgent matters. The communist negotiators protested about American aircraft flying over the neutrality zone and seeking to intimidate those below. Britain deemed the American action unwise and the State Department was told on 21 September that the existence of a neutrality zone presumably included relevant air space. The American air activity stimulated suspicions that the UNC might not be trying hard enough to secure an armistice. Articles in *The Times* near the end of September revealed developing doubt and such suspicion was expressed in private correspondence by a senior official in the Foreign Office [59, p. 243]. The official concerned, Robert Scott, wrote to a colleague in the British embassy in Washington 'that we attach very great importance to securing an armistice in Korea, that we are less pessimistic than the Americans about the chances, that we attach importance also to the way the talks are conducted and to the impression left on world opinion as regards responsibility for the outcome' [59, p. 243].

A general election was held in Britain in October 1951. The Labour government was weakened by the ill health of certain of its leading members and by political divisions resulting from the heavy demands of rearmament on the British economy. Basically the Attlee government was exhausted in consequence of the onerous demands placed on it by major domestic reforms and the Cold War [70, pp. 409–503]. The Labour party won more votes than the Conservatives but the prevailing electoral system produced a small but adequate majority for the Conservative party led by Churchill [109]. The new government was viewed more favourably in the United States. Truman and Acheson respected Attlee but preferred Churchill. The prospect loomed of a closer relationship between the two countries but this was frustrated by persistent strains over the Korean war and, later, over Churchill's wish to secure a measure of *détente* with Russia in 1953. At first Churchill seemed baffled by what he termed 'the humbug and grimaces at Panmunjom' [59, p. 244]. The new foreign secretary, Anthony Eden, was informed by his officials that British views had been conveyed on issues concerning the UNC's air interdiction programme, the use of diplomatic language in the event of a collapse of the talks so that responsibility did not fall on the shoulders of the UNC, and the arguments regarding a line of demarcation.

The principal issues in the armistice negotiations comprised agreeing on a demarcation line, rehabilitation of airfields, and the fate of prisoners of war (POWs). Each side regarded the stance of the other as dubious and designed to strengthen its own position in the case of possible resumption of hostilities on a large scale. The UNC proposed, on 17 November, that the existing line of contact should be the demarcation line. The American joint chiefs of staff were not very optimistic on the likely attainment of an armistice and they did not feel that the UNC should contemplate premature concessions. The British chiefs of staff were more sanguine. Current difficulties centred on suitable supervision terms. It would be impossible to secure comprehensive assurance as regards supervision but this could be balanced through threatening China with tough action. The American joint chiefs considered contingency action against China which could include a naval blockade or bombing airfields and bases in Manchuria; the British chiefs believed that such measures would take too long to have proper effect or would be too dangerous. The most effective action that could be taken against the PRC in Manchuria would centre on the interdiction of communications and eradication of bases and power stations: this would entail fewer risks than implementing a naval blockade of China. Acheson discussed the position with Eden when they met in Rome for a gathering of foreign ministers at the beginning of December. Acheson hoped an armistice agreement could be reached even if supervision did not fulfil wholly satisfactory conditions. A tough warning should be given to the PRC and the DPRK over the dangers of violating an agreement. Eden indicated that Britain would if necessary approve bombing of Chinese airfields, bases and junctions in Manchuria. Britain could not agree to bombing attacks on Chinese urban areas. The British joint intelligence committee considered that the communist states were building up air strength and this would constitute a bigger threat to UNC ground forces: it followed that China and North Korea would want the talks to be as protracted as possible.

Despite the acrid propagandistic mutual insults hurled in Panmunjom, progress was made in the first five months of negotiations [33, pp. 74–107]. This concerned a demarcation line and inspection arrangements; as noted, supervision involved much difficulty. Composition of inspection teams was important and controversial. In February 1952 communist negotiators urged that Poland, Czechoslovakia and the Soviet Union should be members of neutral inspection teams. Understandably the UNC did not regard the suggestion of Soviet membership as one that should be endorsed. It was decided that a wider political conference, with terms of reference to obtain a lasting solution in Korea, should be convened within three months of the signing of an armistice. Rehabilitation of airfields was a difficult issue. The UNC argued that an armistice agreement should contain provisions for banning extension of runways; this would render use by jet aircraft difficult or impossible. New airfields should not be permitted. Exchanges over airfields developed between the two sides in Panmunjom from early December. Agreement accepting the principle of inspection of airfields was reached in December 1951; the communist states proposed inspection by neutral teams. The United States and Britain had anticipated more problems over airfields and the advances made were encouraging.

Prisoners of war

The most intractable problem comprised the ultimate fate and disposition of POWs [33, pp. 108–29]. Originally it was not expected that this would turn out to be the hardest matter to surmount in the armistice deliberations. Why was it so difficult? The principal reason is that moral and political questions merged within it. The Geneva Convention, concluded in 1949, assumed that at the conclusion of a war POWs would be returned to the states for which they fought. Superficially this may have seemed a sound assumption. However, it did not address a contingency in which appreciable numbers of POWs did not want to return to the states for which they fought. The issue was particularly sensitive in the case of the Korean war. Significant numbers of troops who served in the Chinese or North Korean armies had little or no loyalty to those armies. Many Chinese soldiers were simply transferred from Kuomintang armies to communist armies when they surrendered or when their commanders switched sides in the closing stages of the Chinese civil war in 1948–9. Some were converted to communism but others were not. Capture by the UNC afforded them an opportunity to escape and go to Taiwan or elsewhere. Some who served in the NKPA were compelled to enlist in the DPRK or were press-ganged when the NKPA overran the ROK. They now discerned a chance to escape. The Geneva Convention of 1949 was signed but not ratified by the United States. The Chinese communists had not been involved in the negotiation of the convention since China was represented by the Kuomintang regime. The crucial single factor was not the wishes of individual POWs but the decisions that would be taken by political leaders. If all leaders decided that POWs should be returned, in strict adhesion to the Geneva Convention, then this would resolve the matter. If they disagreed, the issue would be highly contentious.

The communist states were adamant that POWs must be returned. To accept the principle of voluntary repatriation would open the floodgates to large numbers possibly deciding that they preferred capitalism or regimes of an anti-communist or non-communist character. Furthermore, it would be a source of deep embarrassment to be forced to admit that newly established communist states did not attract their inhabitants in accordance with communist propaganda. The key leader was the president of the United States. Harry Truman detested communism and coercion. He did not approve of forcibly returning people to states they hated or feared. Truman could recall the anguished scenes in 1945 when Russian POWs were returned compulsorily to the Soviet Union by allied forces. At least in 1945 the Soviet Union had fought as an ally of the United States and Britain from 1941, but the Cold War produced a totally different scene in 1952. Truman saw the moral case as wholly persuasive. In addition, political considerations presented themselves. Truman and his administration endured vigorous attacks, frequently unfair or malicious, for not standing up to communism more successfully. The POW question allowed Truman to claim that he was taking a tough line in defending the rights of those who did not want to live in communist states.

Dean Acheson and the State Department realised that Truman's decision would complicate the task of concluding an armistice agreement, although they did not foresee the extent of the complexity.

The other side of the argument that also required assessment was the fate of UNC POWs in communist hands. Their conditions of imprisonment were harsh: some were dying of malnutrition, disease or maltreatment. Adopting Truman's policy would make it more difficult to obtain their early release: in turn this could give rise to complaints from their relatives and friends. The British Foreign Office responded similarly [59, pp. 248–50]. Civil servants did not expect the situation to develop as it did and thought originally that the Geneva Convention and political realities would prevail over moral arguments. Anthony Eden was influenced to some extent by his officials but deferred to the prime minister. Winston Churchill took the same line as Truman. He admired the president and felt that it would be wrong to diverge from the United States. Therefore, the principle of voluntary repatriation was adopted.

The whole subject of the treatment and fate of POWs was complicated. The issue of principle was straightforward. What was not clear was the actual arrangement for holding POWs in camps in South Korea. When this was clarified in the summer of 1952 it did not provide reassurance. Understandably in one way, the task of guarding camps and superintending them was not assigned high priority by the UNC. Camps were guarded by American and ROK troops. The American commanders did not have enough men to supervise the internal functioning of camps properly. The priority was the military situation and aspects connected directly with the fighting. The number of POWs was large and the camps were dominated by hierarchies of POWs [33, pp. 108–21]. This occurs in most, if not all, gaols of any size to varying extents. The POW camps were a much enlarged version with additional substantial brutality. Camps came to be controlled effectively by hierarchies that were anti-communist or pro-communist, as the case might be. POWs were coerced into declaring a preference whether or not to return to the states for which they fought. Much brutality was used including torture and death. Kuomintang agents were employed as interpreters in some camps holding Chinese POWs and could exert pressure on those they were questioning to say that they did not want to return to the PRC. South Korean agents were also involved in applying pressure in camps holding North Korean POWs. The fact that conditions in the camps were so unsatisfactory emerged in the summer of 1952 in the wake of riots in certain camps. Before the riots the State Department indicated that a smooth process of screening POWs was taking place in a fair manner so that their wishes regarding repatriation could be ascertained accurately. As a result Anthony Eden informed the leaders of the Labour and Liberal parties in Britain, on 1 May 1952, that POWs were treated reasonably and that decisions could be taken without encountering coercion [59, p. 251].

Eden stated that he was fully aware of anxiety felt concerning the treatment of UNC POWs held in communist camps but that the British government felt that forced repatriation of POWs held by the UNC was not acceptable. During the latter half of May ugly riots occurred in camps situated on the island of Koje. This sparked off investigations of conditions in camps more generally and what emerged was highly disturbing. The running of many camps was inept; too much freedom was allowed in the internal functioning of camps, which facilitated the use of coercion by whichever hierarchy of POWs prevailed. The specific incident of Koje included the capture of the American commandant by pro-communist POWs who forced him to state that coercion was used to persuade men to choose in one direction only. Confidence in the process of dis- covering the wishes of POWs was undermined. Press reports and evidence produced by the committee of the International Red Cross caused further doubt and dissatisfaction. Anxiety in the UN increased. Eden was upset that he had received misleading informa- tion from the State Department on the basis of which he had given erroneous assurances in parliament and to party leaders. Eden commented sardonically that public opinion would find it hard to understand how 170 000 men were questioned 'individually and in reasonable privacy' [59, p. 251]. He proposed that a second screen- ing should take place. The high moral tone adopted by the UNC earlier in 1952 was weakened gravely by the revelations from Koje.

The issue of POWs was overshadowed briefly by the UNC's implementation of bombing raids on power stations on the Yalu river on 23 June. The decision was made unilaterally and without consulting Britain or other members of the UN. Embarrassment was accentuated by the fact that the British defence minister was visiting Washington at the time and was not notified. The State Department accepted responsibility for the blunder in not consult- ing Britain. The raids were controversial because they cast doubt on the extent of the UNC's commitment to the armistice talks; in any case, the discussions in Panmunjom were likely to become more difficult in consequence. In Britain the Labour party moved a critical motion. In order to counter the opposition's arguments,

Churchill revealed that the Attlee government had accepted the proposed bombing on the premise that it would be a response to a new Chinese offensive and that consultation occurred beforehand. The revelation achieved Churchill's aim of embarrassing the Labour party and it accentuated growing divisions between left and right in the party.

Within the British Foreign Office certain officials held that too firm a line was being followed over repatriation. Churchill believed that the existing policy must be pursued: it would be wrong to compel POWs to return against their wishes to face torture or death. The situation in the autumn of 1952 was as follows concerning the numbers of POWs and their genuine or alleged preferences. Early in 1952 it was thought that between 10 and 25 per cent of POWs would oppose repatriation. It was estimated that approximately 116 000 out of 132 000 POWs and 18 000 out of 38 000 civilians would go back; approximately 28,000 POWs and 30 000 civilians would oppose forcible repatriation. The outcome of the screening process in April 1952 was that approximately 70 000 desired to return. Subsequently, after further screening, the number choosing repatriation was estimated at 82 000. Ultimately the number repatriated was 82 500: approximately 50 000 decided not to return. Within the UN, anxiety at the prolongation of the armistice talks grew in the summer of 1952. It was one year since the talks began and the initial optimism that a cease-fire would be signed quite soon gave way to gloom and a fear that the war might flare up again or continue for a lengthy period in the existing impasse.

Diplomacy in the UN

The three principal personalities involved in contemplating methods of breaking the impasse were Jawaharlal Nehru, prime minister of India, Lester ('Mike') Pearson, the Canadian minister of external affairs, and Anthony Eden. Nehru had long been critical of American arrogance and overreaction and believed that vigorous efforts were required in the UN General Assembly to secure progress [89; 38]. Pearson was less critical of the Truman administration but concurred that the vexed problem of disposition of POWs must be tackled more imaginatively [75; 58]. Eden felt that voluntary repatriation was justified but too many mistakes had been made by the Americans in dealing with POWs. Eden felt that progress could be achieved in the UN General Assembly, provided that Indian efforts were framed appropriately and pursued diplomatically [9; 59].

Attention therefore switched from Panmunjom to New York in October and November 1952. One complication involved the personality of the Indian delegate to the UN, Krishna Menon. He was mercurial, nervous and unpredictable to deal with. Menon was on good terms with Nehru who entrusted him with the mission of obtaining a solution to the impasse in New York. Menon was distrusted by American officials and regarded as rather exasperating by Eden and his deputy, Selwyn Lloyd. Dean Acheson appreciated that diplomatic pressure on the United States was growing from its allies and those taking a more neutral stance in the UN. Acheson did not handle matters very skilfully. He was weary after a bruising term of office and knew that the impending presidential election in the United States in November 1952 was unlikely to be encouraging for the Democrats. Acheson was critical of the colleagues with whom he negotiated in New York. Menon was seen as erratic and unreliable; Pearson was sententious; and Eden was tedious and had annoying mannerisms. Acheson and Eden in some ways resembled one another in being prima donnas of haughty approach. When Menon first submitted an Indian draft addressing the POW issue, it was regarded by the British as too open-ended and lacking precision. Menon contemplated the creation of a repatriation commission charged with determining classification of POWs according to nationality and domicile. POWs should possess the right to put their arguments before a repatriation commission. The British Foreign Office considered moving to early repatriation based on renunciation of coercion by both sides plus the appointment of neutral nations, with assistance from Red Cross societies, to ensure that agreed terms were followed. The State Department was suspicious of any proposals of imprecise character. Acheson suspected that India in particular and, to some extent, Britain and Canada might be prepared to go too far towards compromise and this would weaken seriously the approach followed by the Truman administration. He did not want further arguments with the joint chiefs of staff apart from which he held that the policy adopted by the Truman administration earlier in 1952 was correct. Acheson disliked the prospect of representatives of Soviet satellite states possessing membership of a neutral commission but this would be unavoidable if a solution was to be reached. Intense negotiations in

New York between the Indian, Canadian and British delegations produced improvements in modifying the original Indian proposal. Eden was encouraged and thought that the United States should show a suitably progressive approach. He was disappointed, for Acheson complained of continuing ambiguity in Menon's proposals as amended: it would be dangerous to allow the communist states to contend that agreement was not being fulfilled.

Further negotiations ensued and these involved Selwyn Lloyd, since Eden had returned temporarily to London. Pearson was the current president of the UN General Assembly. He worked with Lloyd to convince Acheson of the need for compromise but without success. A meeting of representatives of twenty-one states was convened by Acheson on 17 November at which Lloyd urged compromise and forwarding of the modified Indian proposal. Acheson strongly dissented but was consoled only by the support of the Australian and Greek delegates. Far from becoming conciliatory, Acheson proceeded in the opposite direction and sought to persuade Britain to move towards the American position. Eden was annoyed that progress had not occurred and told cabinet colleagues that Acheson was to blame: the secretary of state 'could not have been more rigid, legalistic and difficult' [59, p. 255]. Relations between the American and British delegations in New York deteriorated and each indulged in press leaks aimed at blaming the other for lack of progress. An awkward and embarrassing situation for the UN and for Anglo-American relations was rectified by a most unlikely source – the Soviet Union [9]. Andrei Vyshinsky, the Soviet foreign minister, was present in New York and took a negative line in most of his statements. It had not been expected that Vyshinsky would attack India, since logically it should be in the Soviet interest for India to be cooperating with Britain and Canada in ways disapproved of by the United States. However, Vyshinsky strongly assailed the Indian resolution in a speech delivered in the First Committee of the UN. This afforded Acheson an opportunity to escape from the corner in which he had imprisoned himself. Demonstrating an adroit opportunism, Acheson now applauded Indian endeavours and argued that the Indian resolution, while requiring some modification, was worthy of support. The Soviet Union adhered to the view that conclusion of a cease-fire should be pursued before the POW issue. The Indian resolution was duly carried with the Soviet Union and its allies voting against. The original hope entertained by India, Canada and

Britain that deadlock could be broken was frustrated. The episode was very revealing in showing the strains and tensions within the UN and among the allies of the United States. It was also revealing in demonstrating once more how the communist states could be intransigent at moments when it would have suited their interests to be conciliatory. It was similar to developments in January 1951 when emissaries from the PRC were in New York for discussions with the secretary-general, but China took an unyielding approach when conciliation was required. In this case it is likely that Stalin decided that the idea of voluntary repatriation was not one that the Soviet Union should encourage in any form: this could be very difficult for the Soviet Union at the close of a possible future war in which Soviet forces participated.

Eisenhower's election victory

Attention within the UN and elsewhere switched to assessing the consequences of the American presidential election in November 1952. Twenty years of rule by Democratic presidents ended with the sweeping triumph of General Dwight Eisenhower, the Republican candidate [2; 27]. Eisenhower gained the nomination following a bitter contest against Senator Robert A. Taft, Sr. Eisenhower was an internationalist and held that American global responsibilities must be fulfilled. He possessed great experience of defence matters after a long career in the army. Most recently he had served as NATO commander in Europe. Eisenhower was widely respected and liked, but there were some doubts about his political expertise. Concern in the UN centred on the appointments he would make to important offices and the degree of influence or power that would be exerted by the right wing of the Republican party. Eden met Eisenhower in New York shortly after his victory over Governor Adlai Stevenson. Eden hoped that John Foster Dulles would not be appointed as secretary of state. Although Dulles was an inter-nationalist, he was perceived in Britain as too sinuous an operator and too prone to appease right-wingers in his party. Eisenhower wanted no advice from Eden or any other foreign leader as to who should belong to his administration. Dulles was a man of wide experience who had demonstrated his diplomatic gifts in ably negotiating the Japanese peace treaty in 1950–1: this was the most successful part of American policy in East Asia in the later 1940s or early 1950s. Also Dulles was acceptable to different wings of the Republican party: this would be significant in dealing with Congress. Dulles was duly appointed to the disappointment of Churchill and Eden. Eden persuaded Eisenhower that there was definite merit in Indian attempts to overcome the impasse concerning POWs, contrary to the impression given for so long by Acheson. Eisenhower expressed appreciation and asked Eden to convey this to Nehru [59, p. 256].

There was no chance of securing an armistice agreement in November 1952. The Truman administration was now a 'lame duck' and would soon be departing. All would depend on how Eisenhower and Dulles decided to handle the difficult matters they inherited.

Prisoners of war

We shall end this chapter by considering the experiences of UNC POWs in communist hands. In the successful North Korean offensive at the start of the war significant numbers of American and some British prisoners were captured. They were subjected to brutal treatment, poor food and drink, and savage forced marches in worsening temperatures. The largest numbers of UNC POWs were taken in the period following Chinese entry into the war. Most were captured by Chinese rather than North Korean units: the Chinese treated POWs better in the main. Neither the PRC nor the DPRK signed the Geneva Convention. The official Chinese and North Korean instructions regarding treatment of POWs empha-sised just treatment, but the latter put more emphasis on under-mining the morale of POWs and convincing them of the superiority of communism. The Chinese, too, regarded indoctrination and conversion as important. According to notes taken by a British POW, cited by General Farrar-Hockley, the commandant of a POW camp on the Yalu warned:

After capture, prisoners must be friends and no longer adopt a hostile attitude; they must learn repentance and the meaning of peace. They are lucky to be alive after fighting for the capitalists and they should be grateful that they are prisoners of the Chinese and have the chance to study until they go home The Lenient Policy is unchangeable but there must be no sabotage of study. A hostile attitude to study or any attempt to spoil other students' study will be punished If you are friendly to us you will be treated as a friend, but the Lenient Policy has its limitations as regards our enemies. [29, part 2, p. 267]

Various types of torture were employed against those deemed recalcitrant.

By the summer of 1951 over half of the Americans captured had perished, the majority as prisoners of the North Koreans. At one time the Chinese stated that they had taken 65 000 POWs: at a later stage, they found they held less than 12 000. From the end of 1951 UNC POWs were confined within Chinese–run camps. On the whole, these camps were better run with less resort to savage treatment. Much of each day consisted of political meetings. Extracts from Marxist–Leninist–Maoist writings would be discussed with suitable emphasis on the merits of communism and the evils of capitalism. These extracts were presented drably and evoked few positive responses. The beginning of the armistice talks in July 1951 led to greater care in dealing with POWs with reference to disease and punishment: a higher death rate was not desired. The attempts at indoctrination failed in most cases and POWs proved resilient in exploiting their captors' inadequate knowledge of English in camp entertainments where Chinese rhetorical criticism of their enemies was mimicked. Less direct methods of weakening the resistance of POWs included visits from British communists or sympathisers, such as the journalists Alan Winnington of the *Daily Worker* and Wilfrid Burchett, an Australian who worked for various papers; in addition, Jack Gaster, a lawyer and a member of the British Communist Party, visited camps, as did Monica Felton [29, part 2, pp. 275–6]. The standard of food and supplies improved towards the end of the war in 1953, as the conclusion of an armistice agreement approached.

Communist accusations that the UNC sanctioned use of bacteriological warfare were circulated in 1952 in an endeavour to influence POWs and public opinion in the West [64, pp. 161–3; 91, pp. 275–6]. In the winter of 1950–1 the DPRK condemned the United States for spreading typhus. Subsequently this was replaced with more extensive allegations concerning American resort to bacteriological methods. Allegations appeared in Chinese, North Korean and Soviet publications and media. Specific reference was made to anthrax, bubonic plague and cholera. An international scientific commission was established with communist support to investigate the allegations [29, part 2, pp. 279–80]. One distinguished British member was Dr Joseph Needham, a leading Sinologist, historian of science, medicine and technology in China, and noted for his left-wing political sympathies. The nature of the allegations was broad in scope and the evidence adduced largely comprised statements made by peasants concerning strange events and infected flies appearing after American planes had flown over areas. Of course, much American research was conducted into bacteriological warfare, as was the case in Britain and other countries. The American army was keen to retain Japanese records from odious experiments conducted on POWs in Manchuria during the Pacific war, implemented by the notorious Unit 731. However, convincing evidence was not forthcoming to prove that such weapons had been used in Korea.

Both sides erred in dealing with POWs, particularly in the early stages of capture. The UNC blundered in not attaining far better direction and supervision of camps in the ROK; Kuomintang agents should not have been employed as they were exerting pressure on the Chinese POWs. The Chinese and North Koreans revealed considerable brutality and inhumanity in 1950–1. In the later stages of captivity each side improved its conduct, partly in recognition of previous mistakes made and partly in anticipation of the likely end of the war. However, much would depend on the approach adopted by the Eisenhower administration and on developments in the Soviet Union.

7

The Last Phase of the War and the Signing of an Armistice

Two developments of great importance occurred in the first quarter of 1953. In January Dwight Eisenhower succeeded Harry Truman as president of the United States. In March Josef Stalin died and bequeathed a situation of much uncertainty in the Soviet Union. The more decisive of the two for assisting the signing of an armistice was the demise of Stalin. The foreign policy of Russia was more difficult to predict but it was likely that the new leadership would not want to perpetuate the sterility of the Korean impasse as Stalin had done. The death of Stalin also stimulated Winston Churchill into independent action in a courageous bid to secure a measure of *détente* with Russia [36, pp. 818–33; 109, pp. 55–62].

We turn initially to the arrival of a new administration in Washington. Eisenhower was elected in November 1952 for several reasons, positive and negative. The former included his proven record of achievement in the military and his knowledge of European issues. Eisenhower was one of the few American presidents elected with expertise primarily in the spheres of defence and external policy. He was an attractive campaigner who inspired confidence in the American people. As in all election victories, matters outside his control contributed significantly. The Democrats had been in office for a lengthy period and people wanted a change. Truman's popularity declined steadily following China's entry into the Korean war. The conflict became an albatross around the administration's neck. Truman decided, for personal and political reasons, not to seek a further term in the White House; the man from Missouri would return to Missouri as a genuine 'man of the people'. During the campaign Eisenhower stepped up condemnation of the Truman administration to the ire of the outgoing president. Eisenhower pledged to visit Korea if elected which, curiously, neither Truman nor Acheson had done. He redeemed the promise promptly by flying to Korea at the beginning of December 1952. He met the military commanders for the UNC and acquainted himself with essential features. While not achieving much in practical terms, his visit confirmed the impression formed during the campaign that he was a man of action who did not want to waste time. Eisenhower was a somewhat restless, impatient man [2]. He wished to end the Korean conflict as soon as possible, provided the terms reached fulfilled the criteria laid down. He was disinclined to wait for too long. Eisenhower was under pressure from right-wingers in his party to get tough on communism. The Republicans in the Senate were led by his former rival for the nomination, Senator Robert A. Taft, Sr, from Ohio, and this did not make for the smoothest of relationships. Taft's deputy and successor, William F. Knowland of California, was an 'Asia-firster' and was noted for his enthusiastic, if not fanatical, support for Chiang Kai-shek's regime in Taiwan. The vice-president, Richard M. Nixon of California, had proved an extreme critic of the Truman administration during the campaign and was a friend of Senator Joseph McCarthy of Wisconsin [3]. And McCarthy himself was intensifying his vociferous and wild attacks on communists, alleged communists and alleged sympathisers [78]. Eisenhower had to work with the right wing of his party without becoming its prisoner. Eisenhower's principal biographer, Stephen Ambrose, has shown that Eisenhower disliked many members of his party and fulminated about them in private [2]. However, he veered away from outright confrontation with right-wingers and believed that if McCarthy was given enough rope he would succeed in hanging himself. Ultimately this turned out to be true, since McCarthy eventually destroyed himself politically. But it was a question of how much damage was done to American politics and society in the intervening period. Eisenhower's attitude, while understandable, was not inspiring to moderates, liberals, and those who cared deeply about freedom.

Eisenhower used the National Security Council [NSC] to express his opinions and frustrations to a much greater extent that his predecessor [59, pp. 256–7]. He believed that relentless economic pressure on China, plus encouragement of fears among the Chinese and North Koreans that he might approve the selective use of nuclear weapons, could convince the communist states that an armistice should be signed. A typical assessment by the president in the NSC in the first few months of 1953 comprised an expression of annoyance at the continuing stalemate in Korea; then regret that he could not use tough action to coerce the opposing states; then an appreciation of the apprehension felt in western Europe regarding the danger of a third world war, which could lead to the end of European civilisation. As he had served recently as NATO commander, Eisenhower could understand how sensitive Europeans were to suggestions that atomic weapons should be used in the Korean war or against China. While Eisenhower referred to the possible adoption of nuclear weapons quite frequently, the United States was neither more nor less close to deploying them than at any earlier phase of the conflict. The NSC reviewed the contingency of pursuing a military offensive of very specific character in order to occupy the 'waist' of Korea [59, p. 257]. This would mean taking control of important industrial areas inside North Korea. The enemy would be weakened and there would be tangible benefits for confidence in the Eisenhower administration and for the morale of UNC forces. Following discussion it was decided that the risks of implementing adventurous courses of action were not worth taking as yet.

Churchill's initiative

Relations between the United States and Britain experienced more strain in the spring and summer of 1953. Eisenhower told the NSC in May that he was disturbed over developing arguments with allies concerning policies towards the communist states – 'We were already in considerable difficulties with these allies and, it seemed to the President, our relations with Great Britain had become worse in the last few weeks than at any time since the end of the war' [59, p. 257]. Here Eisenhower was alluding to diverging attitudes between Churchill and himself on how to handle or exploit the aftermath of the death of Stalin. Stalin's iron grip on the Soviet Union and the potent associated fears within and outside Russia of his malign rule ended in March when the old dictator succumbed to the last of a series of strokes. East–West tension could diminish, intensify or remain at around the same level. Western observers differed in their assessments but, in the main, counselled caution and observation. Winston Churchill dissented and followed an interesting and bold approach in the summer of 1953. He enjoyed greater freedom of action because Anthony Eden was away from the Foreign Office for a prolonged period, recovering from a major operation which had nearly killed him. Officials in the Foreign Office were not keen on Churchill's initiative: the same applied to most of Churchill's cabinet colleagues, but they could not prevent him from acting resolutely. Churchill believed strongly that the danger of the Cold War evolving into a global conflict in which the participants would proceed over the precipice, as had occurred in 1914, was very real and urgent action was needed to secure *détente* with Russia. In addition, Churchill's zeal has to be seen in terms of justification for his continued service as prime minister. He was a man with a mission [109]. Churchill viewed the Korean war as one means of reducing tension between East and West. Like Eisenhower, Churchill wanted to conclude the Korean struggle on a satisfactory note: unlike Eisenhower, Churchill believed in cooperating with the Soviet Union to produce this result, since he could not establish direct contact with leaders in China or North Korea.

Originally, when he returned to office in October 1951, Churchill was afraid that the United States might mishandle armistice negotiations and make undesirable concessions simply so as to end the war [59, pp. 244–6]. He changed his mind gradually from the autumn of 1952, probably influenced by the arguments over the Indian resolution to obtain a solution to the interminable wrangle over the disposition of POWs, discussed in the previous chapter. Churchill became more critical of American policy and was unhappy at the American determination to issue the 'greater sanctions statement', immediately after the signing of an armistice. The statement was intended to issue a blunt, unambiguous warning to China of the consequences of breaking an armistice. Churchill saw this as not promoting the more harmonious atmosphere he wished to foster. In Panmunjom, in April 1953, progress was made in agreeing on arrangements for exchanging sick and wounded POWs. In statements made in the House of Commons, Churchill made clear his view that UNC negotiators, led by General William Harrison, should make more effort to reach agreement. Churchill's enthusiasm for achieving swift progress in *détente* was not shared by most in the cabinet but they acquiesced. Eisenhower and Dulles believed that Churchill was acting impetuously and held that it was unwise to pursue too positive an approach: more evidence was required on how the new Soviet leaders would act. Churchill was not deterred by expressions of scepticism and started communicating directly with Molotov who had become Soviet foreign minister again. Churchill told him that the excessive tension of the Cold War should be reduced and that bringing the Korean war to an end would contribute to this objective. Molotov responded positively: while the Soviet Union was not participating in the talks at Panmunjom, 'we can state with satisfaction that the path to a successful conclusion of the negotiations has already been marked out' [59, p. 258].

An obstacle from a familiar quarter appeared at this point. Syngman Rhee intervened to try to prevent the conclusion of an armistice. Rhee consistently opposed signing an armistice on the grounds that it would be a betrayal of the Korean people and would not fulfil the UN's aim of securing a unified Korea. Rhee enjoyed support in right-wing circles in the United States and was well-aware that he possessed considerable nuisance value. He might be fortunate, from his point of view, in blocking an armistice but, if not, he could obtain economic aid and a defence agreement, providing the kind of solid commitment to the ROK which had not existed prior to June 1950. At the same time, Rhee might incur danger if he pushed his opposition too far [91, pp. 330–3]. Eisenhower and Dulles were weary of the Korean war and were determined to terminate it, assuming satisfactory terms were reached. If Rhee was too obdurate, Eisenhower might decide that he was dispensable. A contingency plan was prepared in Washington for instigating a coup to remove Rhee, if absolutely necessary. Rhee was a shrewd operator and appreciated the limits to which he could go. On 18 June Rhee engaged in calculated provocation by releasing 25 000 North Korean POWs from camps guarded by ROK personnel. This action incensed the communist states and the conclusion of an armistice appeared in jeopardy. Churchill acted promptly and contacted Molotov to say that he was convinced that the United States government shared British anger at 'Syngman Rhee's outrage', adding that they must not be deflected 'by this sinister event' [59, pp. 258–9]. Churchill was taken seriously ill on 23 June when he suffered a stroke: the extent of the illness was concealed and Churchill soon resumed dealing with certain business. In the continuing absence of Anthony Eden, the Marquess of Salisbury assumed responsibility for the daily running of the Foreign Office.

The signing of the armistice

Eisenhower and Dulles decided to use diplomatic methods to persuade Rhee to see sense [91, pp. 334–7]. They sent Walter Robertson, an assistant secretary of state for far eastern affairs, to meet Rhee. China and North Korea determined to provide their own appropriate reminder of the exposed nature of his predicament by launching renewed limited military action. Rhee was facing the communist stick and the American carrot with the possibility that an American stick could replace the carrot if he did not compromise. Rhee then agreed to acquiesce reluctantly in the signing of an armistice, but refused to sign himself. In return for his acquiescence, Rhee received economic aid and a guarantee of American defence of the ROK. At long last it seemed that the Korean war was approaching its end, but uncertainty existed until the last moment. On 27 July 1953 an armistice was concluded at Panmunjom. The agreement was signed by Kim Il Sung, on behalf of the DPRK; by P'eng Teh-huai, as commander of the Chinese forces; by General Mark Clark, as head of the UNC; by General Nam Il, as senior delegate of the NKPA; and by General William K. Harrison, as senior delegate of the UN delegation. The preamble stated in part:

> The undersigned ... in the interest of stopping the Korean Conflict, with its great toll of suffering and bloodshed on both sides, and with the objective of establishing an armistice which will insure a complete cessation of hostilities and of all acts of armed force in Korea until a final peace settlement is achieved, do individually, collectively, and mutually agree to accept and to be bound and governed by the conditions and terms of armistice set forth in the following Articles and Paragraphs. [29, part 2, p. 453]

Central features of the agreement included the establishment of a military demarcation line and of a demilitarised zone (Article 1); arrangements for ensuring stability so as to facilitate the convening of a political conference to secure a full settlement (Article 2); the creation of a Military Armistice Commission, meeting at Panmunjom (Article 2B); the establishment of a Neutral Nations Supervisory Commission (NNSC) comprising representatives from Sweden, Switzerland, Poland and Czechoslovakia (Article 2C); arrangements for dealing with POWs, to be discussed below (Article 3); a recommendation from military commanders on both sides that within three months of the signing of the armistice a political conference should be held 'to settle through negotiation the questions of the withdrawal of all foreign forces from Korea, the peaceful settlement of the Korean question' (Article 4).

The provisions for resolving the immediate problems relating to POWs are particularly significant and will now be discussed in more detail. Within sixty days of the signing of the armistice, each side agreed to transfer POWs insisting on repatriation to the side for which they fought when captured. All the remaining POWs were to be released from military control and transferred to the Neutral Neutral Nations Repatriation Commission (NNRC). POWs were to be handed over in Panmunjom: a committee to supervise transfer of POWs was created. Joint Red Cross teams were set up comprising representatives of national Red Cross societies from each of the countries involved in fighting and these teams were to help in the implementation of the agreement relating to the disposition of POWs.

An annex to the armistice pursued the subject of repatriation at some length. Force or threat of force was not permissible in dealing with POWs: they must be free to decide where they wished to go. The NNRC 'shall ensure that prisoners of war shall at all times be treated humanely in accordance with the specific provisions of the Geneva Convention and with the general spirit of that Convention' [29, part 2, pp. 475–6]. POWs declining repatriation would be released from military control and from custody by the side holding them as soon as practicable and definitely within sixty days after signature of the agreement. Detaining forces were responsible for keeping order in areas adjacent to the areas where POWs were held and should act against any irregular forces threatening to cause trouble. Once the NNRC had taken possession of POWs choosing not to be repatriated, arrangements should be made within ninety days for ascertaining the wishes of POWs – 'the nations to which the prisoners of war belong shall have freedom and facilities to send representatives to the locations where such prisoners of war are in custody to explain to all the prisoners of war depending upon these nations their rights and to inform them of any matters relating to their return to their homelands, particularly of their full freedom to return home to lead a peaceful life; [29, part 2, pp. 476–7]. Representatives of the countries concerned should number between five and seven. The NNRC were responsible for deciding the timetable.

All interviews were to be conducted with a representative of each member nation of the NNRC present, plus a representative from the detaining side.

Any POW in the custody of the NNRC wishing to be repatriated would apply to a body comprising a representative of each member state of the NNRC; when an application had been approved, the POW would be transferred to Panmunjom, to be treated in accordance with the procedure stipulated for those undergoing regular repatriation. After a period of ninety days, the issue of disposition of POWs would be forwarded to the political conference. The latter should attempt to reach a decision within thirty days during which time the NNRC would retain custody of POWs. Those POWs electing to go to neutral states would receive help from the NNRC and the Red Cross Society of India. In turn this would be completed within thirty days at which point the NNRC would have fulfilled its terms of reference and would be dissolved. Any civilians who had ceased to be POWs would be assisted by relevant local authorities to return 'to their fatherlands' [29, part 2, p. 479]. India would be responsible for providing essential Red Cross service. The NNRC would provide medical support for POWs. The NNRC should receive logistical support from each side and was responsible for negotiating on local travel arrangements.

The NNRC consisted of representatives from India, Sweden, Switzerland, Poland and Czechoslovakia. India consented to act as chairman, thus accepting what Churchill accurately defined as 'this thankless task' in a message to Nehru [59, p. 261]. The armistice agreement was unclear as to the ultimate fate of POWs refusing repatriation. This was inevitable because of the fundamental disagreement over the voluntary principle. India would play a vital role in determining what happened to POWs in this category. Nehru had followed an independent, conciliatory approach for most of the Korean war. The United States was frequently, if not usually, critical of Indian policy. Now India undertook an extremely sensitive mission in which certain states who had fought in the Korean war were bound to be alienated. The NNRC started to operate on 9 September 1953. India decided that it would not hold POWs, unwilling to be repatriated, indefinitely. Against bitter protests from China and North Korea and criticism from South Korea (which had resented India's independent line during the war), India decided to hand remaining POWs to the UNC. The NNRC completed its task on 29 January 1954 when, according to Indian statistics, a total of 14 227 Chinese and 7582 North Koreans were transferred to the UNC. The Chinese went to Taiwan a week later. Approximately 100 POWs wished to go to a neutral country. Finally, the issue which had delayed the completion of an armistice for so long was settled in January 1954, two and a half years after the opening of armistice negotiations [33, pp. 190–205].

A small number of American and British POWs chose to remain in communist states when the war ended. In a few cases they possessed communist sympathies before the war and in others, they underwent conversion during incarceration. Years later several decided to return to their original countries.

The road to the General Conference

We shall now turn to other aspects of the immediate aftermath of the war. The United States believed it was imperative to issue the 'greater sanctions warning' statement to China, despite British unhappiness. The statement was circulated in the joint policy declarations by the allies on 7 August 1953. On the following day a mutual defence treaty was signed between the United States and the ROK. The future security of South Korea was therefore endorsed with a solid American guarantee which has endured to the present. Increased financial assistance was also promised. Attention now started to focus on the convening of a political conference to agree on a settlement. Nobody could have been sanguine regarding the likelihood of securing a lasting political solution. A civil war was in progress before June 1950 when it was submerged in an international war. With the close of the international conflict, the civil war emerged again. Each Korean state hated the other and was committed to ending the existence of the other when the opportunity occurred. It was impossible to reconcile the ROK and the DPRK. The United States and China were committed deeply, respectively, and could not contemplate a scenario in which the other gained at its expense. The Soviet Union remained committed to the DPRK and could become more committed in the process of emerging rivalry with China for influence in Pyongyang in the years ahead. However, the terms of the armistice envisaged the holding of a peace conference and each side had to take this seriously. Preliminary talks in Panmunjom were not encouraging. The American delegate, a moderate Republican lawyer, Arthur

Dean, walked out of discussions after the Chinese delegate launched a bitter attack on the United States [59, pp. 260–1]. The Berlin conference, held in January 1954, considered further political exchanges designed to take place at a subsequent conference. Agreement was reached between the United States and the Soviet Union that a conference should be held in Geneva in April 1954 to consider a Korean settlement. The American and British governments considered the outlines of a possible settlement which could include a unified, neutralised Korea. Free elections should take place throughout Korea under international supervision, to be followed by the formation of a unified government, developments pointing to neutralisation and withdrawal of foreign forces. Such proposals were unrealistic, for the reasons given earlier.

The Geneva conference assembled in April 1954 [26; 109]. By this time attention in Asia had moved from Korea to Indo-China. The rapid deterioration of the political and military situation facing France rendered obtaining at least a temporary solution in Indo-China more urgent than Korea. The threat of a major war occurring in Indo-China, if the larger powers intervened directly, was more alarming than coping with the political challenges resulting from a war which had just ended. Korea was discussed at Geneva but it was at once obvious that there was no chance of talks succeeding. Relations between the United States and Britain experienced severe strain because of the combination of the extremely negative American attitude, compromise over Indo-China and the high profile adopted by Anthony Eden in working tenaciously for a temporary solution. Eden worked in the spirit of Churchill's earlier desire for *détente* (about which he had been dubious in 1953). Britain and the Soviet Union cooperated as joint chairmen in Geneva and achieved a temporary solution in Indo-China. Korea was shelved as too intractable.

Thus the immediate aftermath of the Korean war may be said to have closed amidst the tranquillity of Lake Geneva in April May 1954. The attention of politicians, diplomats and military men had focused on Korea intensively since the beginning of the conflict. The armistice agreement, signed in July 1953, represented the best that could be hoped for. Both sides knew in June 1951, exactly one year after the war began, that they could not win by military means that were feasible. The armistice talks could have ended sooner if they had been conducted with more skill. It was unfortunate that professional diplomats did not assist prominently in the discussions at Panmunjom instead of military men dominating the exchanges. What was necessary was a mutual appreciation of identifying areas of agreement or convergence instead of harping on about the distinct virtues of rival ideologies and structures. Had it not been for the numerous complexities surrounding the fate of POWs, the armistice talks would have concluded in 1952 instead of 1953. Indeed this was one issue left unresolved when the armistice was signed. India eventually played the key part in solving this most contentious of issues.

8

The Rebuilding of Two Korean States and Continued Enmity

The whole of Korea was one gigantic area of conflict for three years. Devastation, loss of life, grave injuries, missing personnel and separation of families were enormous. Only a very approximate guess at casualties could be made: it is likely that the ROK and the DPRK suffered at least three million killed [42, p. 200]. Armies comprising the two Korean armed services, the UNC's forces (mostly American), and the Chinese army had fought each other savagely for three years. Air battles raged with the Soviet Union joining in covertly. Naval forces operated around the Korean coast with significant Japanese help for the UNC. The extent of suffering was appalling. Poverty was crippling with very low standards of living. No observer, at the end of July 1953, just after the signing of the armistice agreement, would have forecast significant recovery for either Korean state for many years ahead. In fact the aftermath of the Korean war reveals the resilience, dedication and commitment of the Korean people and their leaders to an astonishing degree. Both the ROK and the DPRK became formidable states with tough political leadership [18, pp. 299–495]. For most of the period following the conflict South Korea was governed brutally, with military men determining the character of political and economic advancement. North Korea has experienced harsh, ruthless, dictatorial rule for the entire postwar period. The aim in this chapter is to explore the evolution of the two Koreas since 1953, and to assess the likelihood of ameliorating and perhaps terminating the bitter mutual hostility which had existed since shortly after the end of the Pacific war.

Let us begin with the recovery of the ROK. Syngman Rhee remained president, his pride and obstinacy accentuated by the passage of years. Rhee's aim was unchanged: to secure one unified state, based on trenchant anti-communism and controlled by Rhee and his close supporters. Rhee's autocracy had grown and he was determined that his grip should be tightened and his enemies or critics silenced by one means or another. Rhee was strengthened by the knowledge that the ROK was in receipt of substantial economic aid from the United States and that the defence of the ROK was guaranteed by the presence of American forces. The UN remained committed to the protection of the ROK, although Rhee did not think much of the UN. The biggest single change in the nature of the state in the ROK in the summer of 1953, compared to the situation three years earlier, was the huge expansion in the size and power of the ROK army. In 1950 the army totalled 100 000 men: in 1953 it totalled 600 000 [18, p. 302]. This was a source of strength and weakness to Rhee: the ROK was better able to defend itself but the army could pose a threat to Rhee himself. Time was to demonstrate the truth of the latter point. Rhee needed to develop his power base and reward those who supported or cooperated with him. American aid was channelled into directions that would assist Rhee primarily rather than the ROK. According to statistics cited by Bruce Cumings, the United States provided $12 billion over a period of twenty years. Cumings also cites an alternative estimate that between 1945 and 1976 each Korean, adults and children, received an equivalent of $600 for thirty years [18, pp. 306–7]. American military aid in the 1950s was appreciably higher than for Europe and four times that for the whole of Latin America.

The development of the ROK

In a number of respects Rhee's regime in the 1950s resembled that of Chiang Kai-shek in China in the previous decade. Corruption grew swiftly, as was illustrated in several prominent cases. It would appear that Rhee was not concerned with great personal enrichment but rather with advancing the prosperity of political associates, cabinet officials and hangers-on. Rhee was a very elderly man: while demonstrating considerable political skill, he succumbed increasingly to the temptation of overreaction. This entailed a mixture of corruption, fiddling election results, and employing brutal measures to coerce domestic opposition. One example is Rhee's action in 1958 in arresting one of his former cabinet ministers who had turned against him, Cho Pong-am, and having Cho executed, following a phoney trial [18, p. 343]. The ROK parliament became more divided and raucous as Rhee moved to handicap the opposition. Matters came to a climax in 1960 when a presidential election was held. Student discontent was growing before the election and was accelerated by Rhee's strong-arm methods and electoral chicanery. The opposition candidate died in the United States while being treated for cancer. The election still proceeded and Rhee boasted that he had won approximately 90 per cent of the vote, perhaps not quite what Kim Il Sung could boast of but impressive none the less. Student demonstrations escalated throughout the ROK. As the position deteriorated, Rhee's regime declared martial law. A large crowd advanced on Rhee's official residence on 19 April 1960. Guards opened fire and over one hundred were killed and many more injured [18, p. 344]. The army began to move in and this marked the start of a generation of military dominance in the ROK. Further peaceful demonstrations and discreet but effective pressure from the American embassy in Seoul persuaded Rhee to stand down. On 29 April 1960 Rhee and his Austrian wife departed for Hawaii where Rhee had lived in part during his previous exile. This time, however, it marked the end of his long career, founded on profound obstinacy and deep faith in his ability to unite the Korean people, whether against Japanese imperialism or communism. Rhee's fervent belief in unification was not fulfilled: he died in exile in 1965.

The ROK enjoyed a brief spell of chaotic democracy in 1960–1 with Chang Myon of the Democratic party holding office as prime minister. He represented the landed elite which had opposed Rhee; he was a former ROK ambassador to the United States. Chang was well-intentioned but insufficiently assertive and too deferential to American officials. The weakness of Korea's first taste of democracy, plus the fears of the military that continued lack of firm direction could assist Kim Il Sung's designs, led to the emergence of the 'man on horseback' or, more accurately, in an armoured car. A military coup took place on 16 May 1961, led by General Park Chung Hee. Park came from a humble peasant background and benefited from the Japanese era. He joined the army and received training in Japan, serving subsequently in Manchuria. He worked loyally with the Japanese and was given a decoration by Emperor Hirohito [18, p. 350]. After the events of August 1945 Park transferred his loyalty to the American occupation forces of South Korea. However, in 1946 he participated in a rebellion, leading to suspicions that Park might be a communist sympathiser. He cooperated with the authorities following capture and became sufficiently trusted to be employed in intelligence. Knowledge of his involvement in a past rebellion caused some Americans to suspect that Park might be disloyal. A rumour circulating in South Korea stated that Park had a speedboat situated near Inchon in case the coup failed, but what would have been the destination – Tokyo or Pyongyang [18, p. 350]? The coup's success ensured that Park could create the kind of state he deemed desirable. This proved to be a tough regime, blending military discipline with economic reform. Park remained in power for nearly twenty years. The period witnessed a radical transformation in the economy of the ROK. The foundations for the huge economic success in the 1980s and 1990s (until the setbacks caused by the Asian economic crisis in 1997) were laid by Park's regime. Economic take-off was the product of several developments: substantial American aid, a powerful work ethic, reinforced by Confucianism, and focusing economic growth on the *chaebol*. The latter were the large financial combines which grew rapidly because of the ruthlessness and zeal of their heads and because of military patronage. The *chaebol* began as family groups and the majority have retained this characteristic. Park was influenced by the extensive economic changes he had seen introduced by the Japanese army in Manchuria during the 1930s, the era of rapid industrialisation embracing the military's alliance with the 'new *zaibatsu*' (financial combines).

Park reached agreement with prominent businessmen that he would support them instead of imposing punishment for past collaboration with Rhee's regime, provided that they invested in new industries and collaborated with his government. The *chaebol* strengthened their business ambitions through astute marriage alliances. Park wanted to achieve a strong economy, leading in the second stage to an aggressive exports policy. He did not live to see the full success of the export drive and the start of investment outside Korea but he gave economic development a potent impetus in this direction. Rapid industrialisation was characterised by the same ruthless exploitation of labour seen at the onset of the industrial revolution in Britain and Japan. The work-force was compelled to work long hours for low rewards, often in harsh, deplorable conditions. The workers were recruited from the peasantry and included wide use of female labour. At this time it was easier to coerce the emerging proletariat; later, as prosperity grew in the

1980s, trade unionists became more militant and the industrial pendulum swung towards concessions, comprising material rewards. In the late 1970s economic progress suffered a reverse. Industrial confrontation occurred. Park wished to crack down in the accustomed manner but President Jimmy Carter's administration protested over repressive measures. Carter's intervention encouraged the opposition and demonstrations by workers and students erupted. On 26 October 1979 Park dined with the head of the ROK's CIA, Kim Chae-gyu. A row occurred in the course of the meal; Kim shot Park's bodyguard and then killed Park [18, pp. 374–5]. The motive for the assassination has never emerged: it may be explicable in terms of clashing egos and the power base Kim had created in the CIA. The new ROK leader was General Chun Doo Hwan, head of the Defence Security Council. Chun worked with General Roh Tae Woo to implement a coup within the military which established the power of both men for the rest of the 1980s and into the 1990s. Chun and Roh acted ruthlessly to suppress opposition in the early years of the new regime. The economy revived dramatically in the 1980s and wealth grew at an amazing rate. Demands for democracy became more vocal. Pressure was identified particularly with two courageous politicians, Kim Dae Jung and Kim Young Sam. Both had campaigned for an end to autocracy and military dominance. Kim Dae Jung was cordially hated by the military regime. On one notorious occasion he was kidnapped while in exile in Japan, taken back to South Korea and imprisoned pending execution. Intervention from the United States, Japan and other countries dissuaded the military from proceeding to kill their prisoner. He survived to be elected president of the ROK in December 1997.

Economic progress quickened the growth of political awareness in the ROK. The middle class expanded in size; a significant proportion was converted to Christianity. Developing international communication and travel, together with pressure from the United States, strengthened demands for democracy. The military revealed more flexibility than might have been expected and moves towards a more representative political system occurred. The intention of army leaders was not to advance to democracy but instead to create what might be termed 'guided democracy'. Chun Doo Hwan's fall in 1987 resulted from a combination of serious political unrest, with support from the churches and campaigners for civil rights, plus associated revelations of torture used against student activists. Roh Tae Woo, long friendly with Chun, was chosen to succeed Chun as candidate of the official party in a bid to deflect the discontent. Roh agreed, under American persuasion, to announce changes presaging the adoption of democracy. Direct presidential elections would be held in December 1987 amidst freedom to criticise and campaign; political prisoners were released. Roh was duly elected president because of a fatal split of pro-democracy votes between the two progressive candidates, Kim Dae Jung and Kim Young Sam. In 1989–90 Kim Young Sam decided, together with another leader of a smaller party, Kim Chong-p'il, to join the ruling party in establishing a new party, called the Democratic Liberal party. Kim Young Sam was well placed to succeed Roh and he triumphed in the 1992 election. Although Kim Young Sam had manoeuvred cleverly to gain the presidency, his opportunism possessed deeper significance. He did not come from a military background and was a genuine advocate of democracy. His presidency marked the decline of military power and the ascendancy of democracy.

This was confirmed by Kim's decision to put his two predecessors on trial for implementing the coup in December 1979 and for the bloody suppression of protests at Kwangju in May 1980. Revelations of corruption also played their part. Chun and Roh were found guilty and sent to gaol in 1996. However, they served only a brief period, for they were pardoned shortly before Kim Young Sam retired as president in late 1997. The latter phase of Kim Young Sam's leadership saw the discrediting of the president because of corruption associated with his son. The most serious development concerned the economic repercussions of the Asian economic crisis, which broke suddenly in July 1997. At first this affected Thailand and Indonesia. It then spread elsewhere in South-East Asia and to East Asia. The Korean economy lurched into serious instability, as firms went bankrupt and the danger of economic collapse intensified. The presidential election in December 1997 resulted in a narrow victory for the veteran campaigner, Kim Dae Jung. In political terms his victory was an astonishing confirmation of the changes which had occurred since the late 1980s. For a man who had been condemned to death and hunted in exile, it was a major vindication of all that Kim Dae Jung had worked to accomplish. It must have appeared a poisoned chalice to inherit, given the worsening economic situation. In the early days of the economic crisis Korean leaders and business tycoons expressed defiance and refused to contemplate the unpalatable medicine proposed by the International Monetary Fund [IMF]. However, as the position deteriorated again, Kim Dae Jung undertook to apply the policies recommended by the IMF, which included allowing weaker banks and companies to go bankrupt with resultant rises in unemployment. The vibrant confidence in perpetuating the great economic advances of the 1980s and first six years of the 1990s was shattered abruptly. Both Korean states faced grave crises in 1997–8.

The development of the DPRK

We shall turn next to discuss the evolution of the DPRK from 1953. Kim Il Sung recovered successfully from the failure of his attempt to unify Korea between June and September 1950. He was probably at his most vulnerable later in September and early in October 1950 when it would appear that his critics within the NKWP tried to enlist Chinese help in removing Kim. Thereafter Kim was entrenched in much the way that Syngman Rhee was entrenched as a symbol of the state's determination to survive and revive. Kim's principal rival was the foreign minister, Pak Hon-yong. Pak's power base lay in South Korea: the failure of a significant rebellion within the ROK in June–July 1950 weakened Pak's leadership claims. Other opponents of Kim's included those within the NKWP associated closely with the Soviet Union or China. Kim moved skilfully and decisively to strengthen his power base once the Korean war ended. Pak was arrested, accused of treason for allegedly plotting with the capitalist states, put on trial, condemned and executed in 1955. In the course of the middle and late 1950s Kim acted to remove other opponents and tighten his grip on the party, state and society in general. The cult of the leader grew rapidly. The ideology fostered in the DPRK was termed 'Chuche' (or 'Juche'). This is usually translated as denoting 'self-reliance' in a nationalistic sense. Bruce Cumings has defined it as a method of emphasising the unique features of the North Korean state that resembles Neo-Confucianism rather than Marxism [18, pp. 403–4]. It was an integral part of building the image of the supreme leader, uniquely qualified and gifted to unite and inspire the Korean people. Statues of Kim were erected and loyalty to his leadership was inculcated in the army, industry, among peasants, and in schools and colleges. 'The Great Leader' and father of the people would guide the state away from the perils bequeathed by the Korean war and towards a secure future, which would expand to include South Korea. The latter would eventually see the error of its ways, drop its relationship with hated American capitalism and join in the DPRK to guarantee a glorious future for the Korean people. The unified state would function on the basis of fervent nationalism, combined with Kim's idiosyncratic definition of socialism.

The immediate priority was to rebuild a shattered economy in the DPRK. UNC bombing had caused destruction and devastation and the industrial base of the DPRK was weakened seriously. Bruce Cumings has described developments as 'a serious attempt to construct an independent, self-contained economy' which evolved into 'the most autarkic industrial economy, in the world' [18, p. 419]. Kim's intention was to stimulate the swift growth of a socialist economy-placing the emphasis on heavy industry. The DPRK received considerable assistance from the Soviet Union and China, but the success of its economy, in the first period of twenty years following the Korean war, resulted largely from its own efforts and drive. The industrial base built by Japan was basic to the DPRK's industrial expansion: key figures in industrial development were trained by the Japanese. Some Japanese were retained in 1945 and after to assist with industrial growth. In the late 1940s the economy was advancing fairly successfully, although less so in one or two important industries like coal and metallurgy. Revival and expansion of heavy industries were assigned priority after 1953. Industrial growth probably averaged 25 per cent annually between 1954 and 1964 and around 14 per cent between 1965 and 1978 [18, p. 423]. Growth slowed in the 1970s but remained significant until the early 1980s. Thereafter, the rapid rate of advancement in the ROK outstripped the DPRK. In particular, the DPRK fell seriously behind in the communications revolution. Kim Il Sung carefully avoided being drawn too closely into the Soviet bloc for economic purposes. To have allowed this to occur would have undermined his autarkic aims and in time could have threatened his dominance. In some respects the DPRK lost by not cooperating more closely with Russia; but the progressive disintegration of communist regimes in eastern Europe and the collapse of the Soviet Union in 1991 underline the price that might have been exacted from working intimately with Moscow. By the late 1980s the economy of the DPRK faced grave problems of inefficiency and obsolescence in industry and of falling productivity in agriculture. These were compounded by natural disasters in the 1990s. North Koreans suffered falling living standards in a society never noted for esteeming consumerism. Malnutrition or starvation threatened in the mid-1990s and compelled the DPRK to seek assistance from the West.

The foundations for Kim's ruthless control of the DPRK were the party and the army. The party was purged of his opponents in the later 1950s and Kim faced no challenge from within. Kim relied on old comrades, plus favoured members of his family, to control affairs of state. His son, Kim Jong Il, a product of Kim Il Sung's second marriage, was designated his successor with the title 'Dear Leader'. Kim Jong Il succeeded Kim Il Sung upon the latter's sudden death in July 1994. The DPRK has always possessed a large army: in the 1990s the army comprised approximately one million. The chronic economic difficulties of the DPRK were clearly exacerbated by supporting such a high defence budget. The army was reared on strong doses of '*Chuche*' mixed with hatred of American capitalism which was sustaining the ROK. The Korean war may have ended in July 1953 but the features of a continuing civil war were all too obvious in the tension along the border between the two Koreas; regular acrimonious meetings between the DPRK and UNC delegates have persisted since 1953 and, on a few occasions, physical violence has replaced verbal abuse. Border incidents have been common with mutual accusations of agents being infiltrated for spying purposes or to pursue subversion. The army is on permanent alert and this has inspired frequent apprehension that a new North Korean military offensive to the south could materialise. It is difficult to evaluate accurately the relationship between the leadership and the army since the death of Kim Il Sung. This in turn leads us to ponder the egregious personality of Kim Jong Il. Kim Il Sung's revolutionary credentials were explicit in an impressive curriculum vitae resting on fighting against Japan, working with the Soviet Union in the early years of the DPRK's history, and leading the DPRK through the traumas of the Korean war. *Chuche* provided powerful cement for the charisma. Kim Jong Il's main, or sole, claim to lead the DPRK is that he is his father's son. Therefore, in July 1994 the world witnessed the first transition of power in a communist hereditary state. Little reliable is known about Kim Jong Il. Rumours circulated by those who fled from Pyongyang and talked to South Korean intelligence, who in turn communicated what they desired to appear to the media, indicated that he enjoyed a playboy life style. Certain of the stranger episodes in the external policy of the

DPRK were allegedly linked with Kim Jong Il's ambition, such as the assassination of members of the South Korean cabinet when the latter were visiting Burma in 1983.

When Kim Il Sung died, observers in the West doubted whether Kim Jong Il would survive for long and regarded a military take-over as likely. This has not occurred. However, Kim Jong Il is more heavily dependent on the army than was the case with his father; it is unlikely that the army has the same degree of respect for Kim Jong Il. The DPRK has been an isolated state for most of its existence and a peculiar degree of dedication and self-discipline has been instilled into the people through the educational system, working environment and the armed forces. The DPRK is unlikely to follow the path of swift unravelling which happened in the former Soviet satellite states and in the Soviet Union itself. The DPRK has opened its borders to a limited extent because of the exigencies of the economic crisis. It has been necessary to request or negotiate foreign aid. In addition, there is the lesson of what has occurred in China. In the later 1970s, following the death of Mao Tse-tung, China embraced the market economy with a vengeance and embarked on a process of implementing radically different policies. It was a bold experiment, qualified by an attempt to maintain a state sector, at least for a time, and by determination to retain one political party and to crack down on dissent that became too insistent. North Korea has conducted limited economic experi-ments, influenced by China, but has not gone too far. China is the only country with which the DPRK is on reasonable terms but it is most unlikely that the DPRK, as presently constituted and led, would advance in the way China has done.

Nuclear disputes

This leads us back to consideration of the international role played by the DPRK, including the lively controversy over its nuclear capability. Kim Il Sung demonstrated astuteness in shaping the international position of the DPRK after 1953. He wished to avoid heavy dependence on either the Soviet Union or China. He required their help in the immediate aftermath of war but then he aimed to lessen dependence and to obviate possible Soviet or Chinese intervention in the internal affairs of the DPRK. His policy was flexible and accommodated the necessary adjustments in levels of friendship with Moscow or Peking, according to the needs and realities of the time. The Sino-Soviet split from the late 1950s compelled such readjustment, as Kim inclined towards China. Later he veered back towards Russia. In some respects Kim's manoeuvring resembled that of Tito in Yugoslavia with the major qualification that Kim eschewed contact with the West. However, Kim and Tito were the only independent leaders of communist states outside the Soviet Union and China (until joined by Enver Hoxha of Albania). Kim Il Sung showed interest in nuclear weapons from a comparatively early stage. Since he had lived with the threat of such weapons being deployed in Korea since 1950, this was scarcely surprising. During confidential discussions between representatives of the DPRK and ROK, held in 1972, Kim proposed that if the two states could agree on steps pointing to unification, then they could embark on a joint nuclear development programme. Nothing was achieved in these discussions but the fact that Kim raised the topic is intriguing. A North Korean nuclear plant was constructed in Yongbyon, a town situated about sixty miles from Pyongyang. The attractions of using nuclear power instead of conventional fossil fuels were considerable, especially since the DPRK possessed large deposits of uranium. The Soviet Union provided a small nuclear reactor in 1962. This was expanded from the 1970s through applying the British Calder Hall model of a gas–graphite reactor; this began to function in 1987. American intelligence was aware of the DPRK's programme in broad terms but did not take it too seriously in the 1980s. American alarm grew early in the 1990s, as it came to be appreciated that another Korean war of more deadly nature could erupt [18, p. 466].

American officials and scientists were divided over how dangerous the DPRK's programme was. One interpretation was that the DPRK was using the plant at Yongbyon for diplomatic and economic purposes and did not intend to produce a nuclear bomb. A rival interpretation was that North Korea already possessed a few bombs and intended to produce more. Bruce Cumings argues persuasively that the purpose of constructing a nuclear facility above ground in Yongbyon was to cause maximum speculation and concern in the United States, Japan and the ROK and thus for the DPRK to gain concessions in return for negotiations over the future of Yongbyon. Had the DPRK intended to proceed urgently, much more would have been concealed below ground where it would be more difficult for spy satellites to identify it accurately

[18, pp. 467–8]. Articles appeared in the American press in 1991 speculating on the DPRK's aims and depicting Kim Il Sung as a possible early claimant to the title of principal international troublemaker, vacated temporarily by Saddam Hussein. Tension rose between the United States and the DPRK and the danger of conflict once more occurring in the Korean peninsula was debated more seriously than at any time since the 1950s. The American CIA reported in the latter part of 1991 that the DPRK was on the verge of acquiring nuclear weapons. Other American bodies were less alarmist and maintained that the DPRK would require at least five years to manufacture a bomb. Debate continued in the press and on television throughout 1992. Relations between the DPRK and the United States then worsened rapidly in 1993 and a definite danger of renewed war in Korea existed until October 1994. Both sides acted unwisely. The DPRK stated that it would withdraw from the nuclear non-proliferation treaty. Some American politicians and commentators called for tough action to preempt what British politicians in the 1930s said of Mussolini's ambitions in the Mediterranean region, 'a mad dog act' could be committed by Kim Il Sung. The DPRK's statement was influenced by the American decision to proceed with war games, as part of the regular cooperation between American and ROK forces. In June 1993 the DPRK decided to amend its policy, suspend withdrawal from the nuclear non-proliferation treaty and negotiate with the United States. The talks saw some progress, notably when the DPRK indicated willingness to replace its nuclear programme, utilising natural uranium, with light-water reactors, supplied by the United States. This would facilitate international awareness of the DPRK's capability because it would require supplies of fuel to be obtained elsewhere. However, the situation then lurched in the opposite direction when the DPRK announced closure of its reactor in May 1994. Fortunately Jimmy Carter, the former American president (1977–81) intervened with a most important personal mission to North Korea. Carter met Kim Il Sung and negotiated with him. Carter urged that the DPRK should accept light-water reactors from the United States and suspend its programme. Kim responded positively. Subsequently, in October 1994, it was agreed that the DPRK would suspend its own programme and allow international inspections in return for which the DPRK would receive light-water reactors to advance energy production; loans and credits would be made available to further this objective. It was also agreed that diplomatic contacts between the United States and the DPRK would be strengthened: this pointed to the inauguration of limited semi-formal diplomatic contacts as a possible prelude to full-scale diplomatic relations. An extremely dangerous phase in Korea's postwar experience ended constructively due to the restraint shown by Jimmy Carter and Kim Il Sung. As Cumings has written, the danger of both sides blundering into conflict in 1994 was appreciable and Carter's intervention, as a former president noted for moderate policies, was invaluable [18, pp. 474–7, 484–6]. Kim Il Sung died in July 1994, a few weeks after meeting Carter: Kim's final act in the international arena was conciliatory. Who would have forecast in previous years that the last stage of Kim's leadership, which had endured since 1946, would consist of Kim entertaining a former American president in North Korea? Parallels with Richard Nixon's famous meeting with Mao Tse-tung in Peking in January 1972 spring to mind.

The future

Finally, let us reflect on the past and gaze into the future. In the main, historians are better advised to stick to the past but an assessment of the Korean war and its consequences should include discussion of possible ways of unifying Korea again. Developments in Korea essentially have been determined by the arbitrary division of the country in 1945, by the *de facto* and then *de jure* creation of rival states and by the outcome of the Korean war. The border between the two Koreas varied in 1953 from that obtaining in 1950 but in other respects Korea functioned as before. One important difference in 1953 was the permanent presence of American troops in the peninsula. In the 1990s approximately 38 000 American troops have been stationed in the ROK; between 1957 and 1991 nuclear weapons were kept in the ROK by the United States and could well have been used in the event of war breaking out. Ideally no foreign troops should have remained in Korea after 1953. However, no ideal situation existed, indeed quite the reverse. Given the bitter antagonism between the two Korean states and the prevalent wish in each to see Korea united, it is likely that war would have occurred at the instigation of either state had American troops not been present in Korea. American possession of nuclear weapons may be viewed differently. Introduction of such weapons was contrary to the armistice terms in 1953 [18, p. 477], although it could be argued that their presence strengthened deterrence against aggression from the DPRK. The United States agreed to withdraw the weapons in 1991 as part of a diplomatic exchange with the DPRK.

Prospects for unification

Korean unification could be accomplished in several ways.. Theoretically either Korean state could invade and liquidate the other. Syngman Rhee talked about it, threatened it openly before and after the Korean war, but never implemented it. Kim Il Sung implemented it in 1950, with Stalin's support and with disastrous consequences. Rhee's successors sometimes spoke of advancing north and Kim Il Sung talked of advancing south. Neither side did so but both engaged in provocative acts and gestures. It is very unlikely that the ROK, having evolved into a democracy, would use armed force against the DPRK. It is still possible that the DPRK might attack the ROK. Periodic threats have been made in the 1990s, even when the DPRK has been engaged in discussions with the ROK or the United States. The army is powerful in the DPRK and generals used to operating in a suspicious, isolationist state might decide to launch an invasion. Such a scenario would cause renewed bloodshed and devastation but it would end in the defeat and liquidation of the DPRK. North Korea has no allies to fight for it. The Soviet Union has vanished into history: before disappearing the Soviet Union established diplomatic relations with the ROK. China has also recognised the ROK. Russia would have no interest in becoming involved in a new Korean war. China remains on reasonably friendly terms with the DPRK and has exerted pressure on Pyongyang to compromise during the 1980s and 1990s. But China would have no wish to participate in a conflict in Korea. Therefore, there might be a certain heroism in the DPRK's army advancing with all guns blazing but it would go down to destruction, so that heroism would assume a suicidal character.

Peaceful unification could occur suddenly, over a reasonable time or over a lengthy period. The speed of the collapse of communist regimes in eastern Europe, particularly in East Germany, shows how the process can acquire momentum and direction of its own, once it is under way, and become self-propelling. Clamour from without can reveal the hollowness within. Naturally many comparisons have been made between Germany and Korea, since each was divided arbitrarily at the end of the Second World War and a strong desire for unification affected both. It is unlikely that the DPRK would implode, as happened in the satellite regimes of eastern Europe. North Korea has been isolated to a far greater degree than the latter (except for Albania) and the regimes of Kim Il Sung and Kim Jong Il have maintained much tighter control of society. Most people in the DPRK know comparatively little of the outside world and are unlikely to agitate in significant numbers for democracy. A profound economic crisis could undermine the regime but it is in nobody's interest to see a sudden collapse of the DPRK. The problems would be enormous, far greater than those facing Germany in 1989, and the burden on the ROK would be extremely onerous. It is preferable to contemplate the alternatives.

Kim Il Sung on several occasions suggested a confederal solution. Of course, he was thinking of this happening in a scenario advantageous to the DPRK, not the reverse. Pursuing the confederal path would have certain advantages as well as more obvious difficulties. It would allow the continued existence of both systems with the creation of agreed overall means of achieving one Korea. Time would be granted for a slow process of mutual adjustment, possibly leading to an ultimate merger and the establishment of a fully unified Korea. The drawbacks lie in the retention of features inimical to progress, particularly the size and vested interests of the North Korean army. Animosities could revive again and lead to the disruption of the confederation. Instead it might be more helpful to envisage a process of gradual, agreed cooperation without creating confederal structures. That is to say, issues would be agreed jointly and a procedure or schedule for tackling them determined. The issues to be explored should comprise less controversial matters where agreement could be reached, assuming the basic will to make progress existed. Such issues might include additional food supplies, assistance for agriculture and industry, and arrangements for families, separated through the creation of the two states, to meet regularly. Nuclear matters, discussed above, could furnish a basis for additional progress. A vital aspect would be to diminish the international isolation of the DPRK and to secure working diplomatic relationships between the DPRK and as many countries as possible. The DPRK joined the UN in 1991 and it should have positive relations with its fellow members. The most important would be with the United States. The remaining bitterness resulting from the war of 1950–3 could be dissipated and a point reached where American forces could be withdrawn from Korea. Eventually, over a substantial period, defined as medium- to long-term, agreement could be attained for unification with the creation of one government, elected democratically. This would assume that institutions changed gradually in the DPRK and that *Chuche* diminished to connote a less aggressive expression of faith and reliance in Korean values. The army would remain as a major obstacle, perhaps *the* obstacle. The tenacity of martial tradition and the size of the armed forces would be a severe test of cooperation. Many soldiers would have to transfer to civilian work; this would also apply to the ROK army. There is experience in other countries or areas of bringing together rival military groups or armies, as in colonies approaching independence or in South Africa, following the collapse of the apartheid regime. Some of this experience is not encouraging but progress has been made in a significant number of cases.

Conclusions

Civil wars are notoriously the worst conflicts to contemplate. The American civil war of 1861–5, the Irish civil war of 1922–3 and the Spanish civil war of 1936–9 afford horrific examples. The harsh divisions within families and between friends or colleagues engender savagery of peculiar intensity. Korea has suffered the rigours and traumas of a profoundly divided society since 1945, if not 1910. Deep hostility has existed between the ROK and DPRK for half a century: the situation has been that of a civil war, bubbling away, constrained from erupting fully, except between 1950 and 1953. The civil war then merged with an international war. A conflict of the kind that developed in 1950 was desired by no one but error and miscalculation led it to expand until the UN was committed heavily as an organisation with sixteen of its members sending personnel to Korea; to this has to be added the direct intervention of China, the indirect intervention of the Soviet Union, and the deployment of Japanese forces and equipment under American direction. The international war could have been avoided had the United States and the Soviet Union acted with greater clarity and circumspection. The Truman administration should have made it clear that South

Korea would be defended in the event of attack. Had this been stated unequivocally between the summer of 1948 and the spring of 1950, then it is most unlikely that the Soviet Union would have encouraged Kim Il Sung to advance. The United States made no such statement for two reasons: Korea was not the chief priority, Europe was, and the Truman administration distrusted Syngman Rhee. Given any degree of encouragement, Rhee might launch an invasion of the DPRK. A firmer strategy for dealing with Rhee, of the kind followed by the Eisenhower administration in the 1950s after the war ended, could have worked successfully. Stalin erred badly in acceding to Kim Il Sung's request for support and departing from the caution previously shown. The Korean war embroiled the United States and China, which Stalin doubtless welcomed, but it also marked a huge increase in American rearmament and a powerful increase in American preparedness for conflict against the Soviet Union. The American commitment to Europe was strengthened. The Korean war probably helped General Eisenhower secure the Republican party's nomination for the presidency in 1952 which was not in Stalin's interest. Indeed, from a long perspective, it could be said that Stalin's miscalculation in 1950 accentuated the budgetary problems of the Soviet Union so dangerously that ultimately the Soviet Union collapsed because of the unsustainable burden falling on its economy.

The inability to conclude a peace settlement in 1953–4 perpetuated a dangerous, unstable situation. War could easily have broken out again and it could still occur. That it has not recurred is attributable to two factors: the recollection of what did happen between 1950 and 1953 and luck. The two combined, as in 1994, ensured that savage conflict did not engulf the Korean people and American forces once more. There is no guarantee that luck would prevail if the DPRK felt so vulnerable and threatened that its army regarded offensive action as the answer to its oppressive dilemmas.

Appendix: Fighting Prowess – the achievements and failings of each side during the Korean war

Each side had experienced significant achievements and defects in its fighting record during the conflict in Korea between 1950 and 1953. The army of the DPRK (North Korea) demonstrated tenacity and dedication in its bold advance in June–July 1950: the same qualities were shown in the regrouping, following the severe setback inflicted by the UNC in September–October 1950. The combination of practical experience as guerrillas fighting against the Japanese, of fighting as part of the Chinese communist forces and of receiving Soviet training and direction resulted in an army of considerable vigour and ruthlessness. In June 1950 it comprised total fighting forces of approximately 152 000, most being in the army. The navy and air force constituted sections of the NKPA: both were small, the navy comprising miscellaneous former Russian, German and Japanese vessels, and the air force consisting of 78 YAK-7B fighters and 70 Il-10 bombers.

The People's Liberation Army of China possessed vast numbers, which rendered it easier for Mao Tse-tung to contemplate losses on a significant scale. The army was imbued with confidence and zeal, arising from its remarkable achievement in securing the comprehensive rout of the Kuomintang forces in the Chinese civil war (1946–9). P'eng Teh-huai, who commanded the Chinese forces in Korea, was a leader of experience and courage, well-suited to the post he occupied. The principal contribution of the Chinese lay in the extremely humiliating defeat imposed on the UNC forces between November 1950 and February 1951. The Chinese communist army proved that it was a formidable body and that China was a power to be reckoned with in eastern Asia. The weaknesses of the army comprised logistical difficulties, accentuated by the long drive down the Korean peninsula in pursuit of the retreating UNC forces, plus inferior weapons, equipment and clothing. Chinese air power was weak but was bolstered by the covert air assistance provided by the Soviet Union. Chinese pilots operated the bulk of the aircraft supplied by Russia. Chinese troops relied in part upon seizing the psychological initiative rapidly: this was accomplished through the skilful use of bugles and gongs, particularly at night. P'eng Teh-huai was able and resourceful: while originally rather too optimistic on what could be accomplished, he subsequently displayed greater realism than Mao Tse-tung who persisted in believing, until the summer of 1951, that it would be possible to dictate the terms of a settlement to the UNC. The Chinese troops gained the respect of their opponents for their dedication and courage. Chinese officers treated POWs with some restraint and without the degree of cruelty frequently shown by the North Koreans.

The Soviet Union did not participate directly in the war. However, Soviet officers contributed significantly to the preparation of the initial DPRK offensive in June 1950, although Stalin ordered the withdrawal of military personnel shortly after the start of the war, once it became clear that the United States would commit itself to direct intervention in Korea. The bulk of equipment and war material was provided by the Soviet Union in order to sustain China and the DPRK throughout the war. The most important single aspect of Soviet assistance concerned air power. MIG-15 fighters and transport aircraft were vital to communist resistance in the air. Stalin authorised the use of Soviet pilots on condition that they wore Chinese uniforms and that their role remained covert. The extent of Soviet air action emerged in full only a generation after the end of the Korean war. MIG-15 fighters first appeared in November 1950, causing much alarm within the UNC. By the summer of 1951 over 400 MIG-15s were participating: by 1953 this figure had doubled. Stalin's aims were to obviate the liquidation of the DPRK in the autumn of 1950 and then to prevent an armistice being signed, unless the communist side could emerge with some clear gains.

The army of the ROK (South Korea) was not equipped to fight a major war in June 1950. It lacked tanks and air power. Although a large American military mission operated in the ROK, American policy towards the ROK was ambivalent. The total armed forces of the ROK in June 1950 stood at approximately 104 000, including the coast guard and the members of the nominal air force. Some units of the ROK army fought effectively but the general picture was one of poor leadership, tactics and morale. American military intervention stiffened the morale of the ROK army and an improvement in its performance occurred in the autumn of 1950, following the successful landing of UNC troops at Inchon. But the ROK army once again behaved disappointingly in response to the first direct Chinese military action late in October 1950. The temporary decline in American military morale late in 1950 and early in 1951 threatened to undermine the ROK army. However, General Ridgway's success in rebuilding the confidence of American forces assisted gradual stabilisation of the ROK army. The latter was further strengthened in the later stages of the war but the task of achieving an army of markedly higher expertise and effectiveness was a challenge to be met in the postwar period.

The military record of the United States in Korea was mixed and, on balance, was not as effective as the achievements of the American armed forces in the Second World War would have led one to anticipate. The explanation lies in a combination of factors. The speed of the reduction in the size of the United States army after 1945 involved the departure or retirement of experienced officers. The American occupation forces in Japan tended to develop a comfortable, relaxed lifestyle which was not conducive to a swift translation into a conflict of savage proportions in Korea. The initial performance of American troops was disappointing in July–August 1950. The ensuing period saw a dramatic but, as it turned out, deceptive improvement, as the DPRK army fell back rapidly and the United States Eighth Army advanced at a hectic pace. Chinese intervention led to the worst phase of the war for the United States and the UN. General MacArthur permitted an excessively fast retreat back down the Korean peninsula. Some American officers and men demonstrated resilient qualities amidst great adversity but the overall picture was bad. Eyewitness reports included such features as panic, desertion, and failure to support wounded or injured men. Individual American officers were appalled at what they witnessed and more than a generation later found the situation very difficult or impossible to explain. The credit in rectifying the position belonged to General Ridgway who took a tough line in dealing with incompetent or weak officers and instilled a new vigour and determination through his own fearless example. The removal of MacArthur in April 1951 improved matters through eliminating the chronic divergence between the Truman administration in

Washington, DC, and the most senior American – and UN – commander. American military confidence and competence were restored in 1951 to the point where the United States army could hold the territory occupied until an armistice agreement was signed. The American forces committed to action in Korea consisted of the Eighth Army with six army divisions and one marine division, three naval task forces and three air forces.

In the air and at sea American might, supplemented by its allies in the UNC, prevailed. Before the war began, and for a fleeting period just after it began, it had been believed that the deployment of air power could halt a North Korean advance successfully. Interestingly, this feeling emerged again in the spring and summer of 1951. The gravity of the crisis in late June 1950 proved that only the deployment of sizeable ground forces could stop the DPRK. However, the United States soon established command of the air and this was retained throughout the war, subject to noting the serious challenge coming from MIG-15 fighters once the Soviet Union extended assistance to China and the DPRK. The early American fighter plane, the F-80 Shooting Star, proved inadequate in combating the MIG-15s. However the Sabre, F86, was successful in containing the challenge from the MIG-15s; the problem was that the Sabres could be provided only in relatively small numbers, owing to heavy demand in other parts of the world. Despite the latter difficulty, the Sabres ensured UNC dominance in the air. American bombing of the DPRK was extensive and resulted in considerable devastation and suffering. At sea the United States, with British assistance, possessed effective control: British naval help was of importance at the beginning of the war, before the American fleet arrived. Japanese assistance in naval operations is of interest in revealing the United States encouraging violation of the terms of the Japanese constitution of 1946.

The United Nations was committed for the first time to military action by member states in order to defeat an act of aggression which had been condemned formally in the UN Security Council. Only one country contributed forces of any size, apart from the United States. Great Britain contributed two infantry brigades, one armoured regiment, one and a half engineer regiments with concomitant ground forces, all functioning as part of the First Commonwealth Division, plus the Far Eastern fleet and Sunderland aircraft of the Royal Air Force. British troops fought stubbornly and courageously: they acted less flamboyantly than the Americans but with greater stability than their American colleagues. This was illustrated most graphically in the fast-changing events between November 1950 and February 1951.

The other member states of the UN to contribute were Australia, Belgium, Canada, Colombia, Ethiopia, France, Greece, Luxembourg, the Netherlands, New Zealand, the Philippines, Thailand, Turkey and the Union of South Africa. Medical units were provided by Denmark, Italy, India, Norway and Sweden. However, the role of the UN was fulfilled in the main by the United States; the UNC was in essence a vehicle for securing American military objectives.

Bibliography

Please note that items are numbered in accordance with the numbers used in the body of the text.

1. ACHESON, Dean, *Present at the Creation: My Years in the State Department* (London: Hamish Hamilton, 1970).
2. AMBROSE, Stephen, *Eisenhower*, 2 vols (London: Allen & Unwin, 1983–4).
3. AMBROSE, Stephen, *Nixon*, Vol. I, *The Education of a Politician, 1913–1962* (London: Simon & Schuster, 1987).
4. APPLEMAN, Roy E., *South of the Naktong, North to the Yalu* (Washington, DC: Office of the Chief of Military History, 1961).
5. BAILEY, Sydney D., *The Korean Armistice* (New York: St Martin's Press, 1992).
6. BLUM, Robert M., *Drawing the Line: The Origin of American Containment Policy in East Asia* (London: Norton, 1982).
7. BUCKLEY, Roger D., *Occupation Diplomacy: Britain, the United States and Japan 1945–1952* (Cambridge: Cambridge University Press, 1982).
8. BUCKLEY, Roger, D., *U.S.–Japan Alliance Diplomacy, 1945–1990* (Cambridge: Cambridge University Press, 1992).
9. BULLEN, Roger, 'Great Britain, the United States and the Indian Armistice Resolution on the Korean War, November 1952', in Ian Nish (ed.), *Aspects of Anglo–Korean Relations* (London: STICERD, London School of Economics, 1984), pp. 27–44.
10. BULLOCK, Alan, *The Life and Times of Ernest Bevin*, Vol. III, *Foreign Secretary, 1945–1951* (London: Heinemann, 1983).
11. CARIDI, Ronald, *The Korean War and American Politics: The Republican Party as a Case Study* (Philadelphia: University of Pennsylvania Press, 1968).

123

12. CHANG, Gordon H., *Friends and Enemies: The United States, China, the Soviet Union, 1948–1972* (Stanford, Calif.: Stanford University Press, 1990).

13. CHEN, Jian, *China's Road to the Korean War: The Making of the Sino-American Confrontation* (New York: Columbia University Press, 1994).

14. CLAYTON, David, *Imperialism Revisited: Political and Economic Relations between Britain and China, 1950–54* (London: Macmillan, 1997).

15. COTTON, James and NEARY, Ian [eds], *The Korean War in History* (Manchester: Manchester University Press, 1989).

16. CUMINGS, Bruce, *The Origins of the Korean War*, Vol. I, *Liberation and the Emergence of Separate Regimes, 1945–1947* (Princeton, NJ: Princeton University Press, 1981).

17. CUMINGS, Bruce, *The Origins of the Korean War*, Vol. II, *The Roaring of the Cataract, 1947–1950* (Princeton, NJ: Princeton University Press, 1990).

18. CUMINGS, Bruce, *Korea's Place in the Sun: A Modern History* (London: Norton, 1997).

19. CUMINGS, Bruce (ed.), *Child of Conflict: the Korean–American Relationship, 1943–1953* (Seattle: University of Washington Press, 1983).

20. DINGMAN, Roger, 'Atomic Diplomacy during the Korean War', *International Security*, vol. 13, no. 3 (1988–9), pp. 50–91.

21. DOCKRILL, Michael, 'The Foreign Office, Anglo–American Relations and the Korean War, June 1950–June 1951', *International Affairs*, Vol. 62 (1986), pp. 459–76.

22. DOCKRILL, Michael and YOUNG, J. W. (eds), *British Foreign Policy, 1945–56* (London: Macmillan, 1989).

23. DONOVAN, Robert J., *Tumultuous Years: The Presidency of Harry S. Truman, 1949–1953* (London: Norton, 1982).

24. DOWER, John W., *Empire and Aftermath: Yoshida Shigeru and the Japanese Experience, 1878–1954* (Cambridge, Mass.: Harvard University Press, 1979).

25. DRIFTE, Reinhard, *The Security Factor in Japan's Foreign Policy, 1945–1952* (Ripe, East Sussex: Saltire Press, 1983).

26. EDEN, Anthony (Earl of Avon), *Memoirs: Full Circle* (London: Cassell, 1960).

27. EISENHOWER, Dwight D., *Memoirs*, Vol. I, *Mandate for Change* (New York: Doubleday & Company, 1963).

28. FARRAR, Peter N., 'Britain's Proposal for a Buffer Zone South of the Yalu in November 1950', *Journal of Contemporary History*, Vol. 18, no. 2 (1983), pp. 327–51.
29. FARRAR-HOCKLEY, Anthony, *The British Part in the Korean War*, 2 parts (London: HMSO, 1990–5).
30. FENG, Zhong-Ping, *The British Government's China Policy, 1945–1950* (Keele: Keele University Press, 1994).
31. FINN, Richard B., *Winners in Peace: MacArthur, Yoshida and Postwar Japan* (Oxford; University of California Press, 1992).
32. FOOT, Rosemary, *The Wrong War: American Policy and the Dimensions of the Korean Conflict, 1950–1953* (London: Cornell University Press, 1985).
33. FOOT, Rosemary, *A Substitute for Victory: The Politics of Peacemaking and the Korean Armistice Talks* (London: Cornell University Press, 1990).
34. FOOT, Rosemary, *The Practice of Power: U.S. Relations with China since 1949* (Oxford: Oxford University Press, 1995).
35. GADDIS, John, *Strategies of Containment* (Oxford: Oxford University Press, 1982).
36. GILBERT, Martin, *Winston S. Churchill*, Vol. VII (London: Heinemann, 1988).
37. GONCHAROV, Sergei N., LEWIS, John W. and XUE, Litai, *Uncertain Partners: Stalin, Mao and the Korean War* (Stanford, Calif.: Stanford University Press, 1994).
38. GOPAL, Sarvepalli, *Jawaharlal Nehru: A Biography*, Vol. II, *1947–1956* (London: Jonathan Cape, 1979).
39. GORDENKER, Leon, *The United Nations and the Peaceful Unification of Korea: The Politics of Field Operations, 1947–1950* (The Hague: Martinus Nijhoff, 1959).
40. GRAJDANZEV, Andrew J., *Modern Korea* (New York: Institute of Pacific Relations, John Day Company, 1944).
41. GROMYKO, Andrei, *Memories* (London: Hutchinson, 1989).
42. HALLIDAY, Jon and CUMINGS, Bruce, *Korea: The Unknown War* (London: Viking, 1988).
43. HAMBY, Alonzo L., *Man of the People: A Life of Harry S. Truman* (Oxford: Oxford University Press, 1996).
44. HASTINGS, Max, *The Korean War* (London: Simon & Schuster, 1988).
45. HENDERSON, Gregory, *Korea: The Politics of the Vortex* (Cambridge, Mass.: Harvard University Press, 1968).

46. HERSHBERG, James G. (ed.), *The Cold War in Asia*, the Cold War International History Project Bulletin, Issues 6–7 (Washington, DC: Woodrow Wilson International Center, 1996).

47. HOGAN, Michael J., *The Marshall Plan: America, Britain and the Reconstruction of Western Europe, 1947–1952* (Cambridge: Cambridge University Press, 1987).

48. HOLLOWAY, David, *Stalin and the Bomb: The Soviet Union and Atomic Energy, 1939–1956* (London: Yale University Press, 1994).

49. JAMES, D. Clayton, *The Years of MacArthur*, Vol. III, *Triumph and Disaster, 1945–1964* (Boston, Mass.: Houghton Mifflin, 1985).

50. JAMES, Robert Rhodes, *Anthony Eden* (London: Weidenfeld & Nicolson, 1986).

51. JOY, C. Turner, *Negotiating While Fighting: The Diary of Admiral C. Turner Joy at the Korean Armistice Conference* (Stanford, Calif.: Hoover Institution Press, 1978).

52. KENNAN, George, *Memoirs, 1925–1950* (London: Hutchinson, 1968).

53. KENNAN, George, *Memoirs, 1950–1963* (Boston: Little, Brown, 1972).

54. KHRUSHCHEV, Nikita S., *Khrushchev Remembers* (London: André Deutsch, 1971).

55. KIM, Joungwon A., *Divided Korea: The Politics of Development, 1945–1972* (Cambridge, Mass.: Harvard University Press, 1976).

56. KOLKO, Joyce and Gabriel, *The Limits of Power: The World and United States Foreign Policy, 1945–1954* (London: Harper & Row, 1972).

57. LARGE, Stephen, *Emperor Hirohito and Showa Japan* (London: Routledge, 1992).

58. LEE, Steven Hugh, *Outposts of Empire: Korea, Vietnam and the Origins of the Cold War in Asia, 1949–1954* (Liverpool: Liverpool University Press, 1995).

59. LOWE, Peter, *Containing the Cold War in East Asia: British Policies towards Japan, China and Korea, 1948–1953* (Manchester: Manchester University Press, 1997).

60. LOWE, Peter, *The Origins of the Korean War*, 2nd edn (London: Longman, 1997).

61. LOWE, Peter, 'An Ally and a Recalcitrant General: Great Britain, Douglas MacArthur and the Korean War, 1950–1', *English Historical Review*, vol. 105, no. 416 (1990), pp. 624–53.

62. LUARD, Evan, *A History of the United Nations*, Vol. I, *The Years of Western Domination, 1945–1955* (London: Macmillan, 1982).
63. MacARTHUR, Douglas, *Reminiscences*, paperback edition (Greenwich, Conn.: Fawcett Publications Inc., 1965).
64. MacDONALD, Callum, *Korea: The War before Vietnam* (London: Macmillan, 1986).
65. MacDONALD, Callum, 'The Atomic Bomb and the Korean War, 1950–53', in Dick Richardson and Glyn Stone [eds], *Decisions and Diplomacy: Essays in Twentieth Century International History: In Memory of George Grün and Esmonde Robertson* (London: Macmillan, 1995), pp. 174–204.
66. McGIBBON, Ian, *New Zealand and the Korean War*, Vol I, *Politics and Diplomacy* (Auckland: Oxford University Press, in association with the Historical Branch, Department of Internal Affairs, 1993).
67. McGLOTHLEN, Ronald, *Controlling the Waves: Dean Acheson and U.S. Foreign Policy in Asia* (London: Norton, 1993).
68. McINTYRE, W. David, *Background to the ANZUS Pact: Policy–Making, Strategy and Diplomacy, 1945–55* (London: Macmillan, 1995).
69. MERRILL, John, *Korea: The Peninsular Origins of the War* (London: Associated University Presses, 1989).
70. MORGAN, Kenneth O., *Labour in Power, 1945–1951* (Oxford: Clarendon Press, 1984).
71. NAGAI, Yonnosuke and IRIYE, Akira (eds), *The Origins of the Cold War in Asia* (Tokyo: University of Tokyo Press, 1977).
72. OLIVER, Robert T., *Syngman Rhee and American Involvement in Korea, 1942–1960* (Seoul: Panmun Books, 1960).
73. O'NEILL, Robert, *Australia in the Korean War, 1950–53*, Vol. I, *Strategy and Diplomacy* (Canberra: The Australian War Memorial and the Australian Government Publishing Service, 1981).
74. OVENDALE, Ritchie, *The English–Speaking Alliance: Britain, the United States, the Dominions, and the Cold War* (London: Allen & Unwin, 1985).
75. PEARSON, Lester, *Mike: The Memoirs of the Right Honourable Lester B. Pearson*, Vol. II, *1948–1957*, ed. John A. Munro and Alex I. Inglis (Toronto: University of Toronto Press, 1973).
76. PENG, Dehuai, *Memoirs of a Chinese Marshal: A Cultural Revolution 'Confession' by Marshal Peng Dehuai (1893–1974)* (Peking: Foreign Languages Press, 1984).

77. REES, David, *Korea: The Limited War* (London: Macmillan, 1964).
78. REEVES, Thomas C., *The Life and Times of Joe McCarthy: A Biography* (London: Blond & Briggs, 1982).
79. RIDGWAY, Matthew B., *The War in Korea* (London: Barrie & Rockcliffe/The Cresset Press, 1967).
80. SCALAPINO, Robert A. and LEE, Chong-sik, *Communism in Korea*, 2 parts (Berkeley: University of California Press, 1972).
81. SCHALLER, Michael, *Douglas MacArthur: The Far Eastern General* (Oxford: Oxford University Press, 1989).
82. SCHNABEL, James E. and WATSON, Robert J., *The History of the Joint Chiefs of Staff*, 4 vols (Wilmington, Del.: Michael Glazier, 1979).
83. SCHONBERGER, Howard B., *Aftermath of War: Americans and the Remaking of Japan, 1945–1952* (London: Kent State University Press, 1989).
84. SCHRAM, Stuart R., *Mao Zedong: A Preliminary Reassessment* (Hong Kong: Chinese University Press, 1983).
85. SHAO, Wenguang, *China, Britain and Businessmen: Political and Commercial Relations, 1949–57* (London and Oxford: Macmillan/St Antony's College, 1991).
86. SHLAIM, Avi, *The United States and the Berlin Blockade, 1948–1949: A Study in Crisis Decision-Making* (London: University of California Press, 1983).
87. SHORT, Anthony, *The Communist Insurrection in Malaya, 1948–1960* (London: Frederick Muller, 1975).
88. SIMMONS, Robert R., *The Strained Alliance: Peking, Pyongyang, Moscow and the Politics of the Korean Civil War* (London: Collier-Macmillan, 1975).
89. SINGH, Anita Inder, *The Limits of British Influence: South Asia and the Anglo-American Relationship, 1947–56* (London: Pinter, 1993).
90. STEPHAN, J. J., *The Russian Far East: A History* (Stanford, Calif.: Stanford University Press, 1995).
91. STUECK, William, *The Korean War: An International History* (Princeton, NJ: Princeton University Press, 1995).
92. SUH, Dae–sook, *Kim Il Sung: The North Korean Leader* (New York: Columbia University Press, 1988).
93. SUH, Dae-sook, *The Korean Communist Movement, 1918–1948* (Princeton, NJ: Princeton University Press, 1967).

94. SUH, Dae-sook (ed.), *Documents of Korean Communism, 1918–1948* (Princeton, NJ: Princeton University Press, 1970).
95. TANG, James Tuck-Hong, *Britain's Encounter with Revolutionary China, 1949–54* (London: Macmillan, 1992).
96. THORNE, Christopher, *Allies of a Kind: The United States, Britain and the War against Japan, 1941–45* (London: Hamish Hamilton, 1978).
97. TROTTER, Ann, *New Zealand and Japan, 1945–1952: The Occupation and the Peace Treaty* (London: Athlone Press, 1990).
98. TRUMAN, Harry S., *Memoirs: Year of Decisions, 1945* and *Years of Trial and Hope, 1946–52*, paperback edition (New York: Signet Books, 1965).
99. TSANG, Steve (ed.), *In the Shadow of China: Political Developments in Taiwan since 1949* (London: Hurst, 1993).
100. TUCKER, Nancy B., *Patterns in the Dust: Chinese–American Relations and the Recognition Controversy, 1949 1950* (New York: Columbia University Press, 1983).
101. VAN REE, Erik, *Socialism in One Zone: Stalin's Policy in Korea, 1945–1947* (Oxford: Berg, 1989).
102. WEATHERSBY, Kathryn, *Soviet Aims in Korea and the Origins of the Korean War, 1945–1950: New Evidence from Russian Archives*, Cold War International History Project (Washington, DC: Woodrow Wilson International Center for Scholars, 1993).
103. WEATHERSBY, Kathryn, 'The Soviet Role in the Early Phase of the Korean War: New Documentary Evidence', *Journal of American–East Asian Relations*, vol. III (1994), pp. 1–33.
104. WELFIELD, John, *An Empire in Eclipse: Japan in the Postwar American Alliance System* (London: Athlone Press, 1988).
105. WHITING, Allen S., *China Crosses the Yalu: The Decision to Enter the Korean War* (London: Macmillan, 1960).
106. WILLIAMS, William J. (ed.), *A Revolutionary War: Korea and the Transformation of the Postwar World* (Chicago: Imprint Publications, 1993).
107. YOSHITSU, Michael M., *Japan and the San Francisco Peace Settlement* (New York: Columbia University Press, 1983).

108. YOUNG, John W. (ed.), *The Foreign Policy of Churchill's Peacetime Administration, 1951–1955* (Leicester: Leicester University Press, 1988).
109. YOUNG, John W., *The Longman Companion to Cold War and Détente, 1941–91* (London: Longman, 1993).
110. ZHAI, Qiang, *The Dragon, the Lion and the Eagle: Chinese–British–American Relations, 1949–1958* (London: Kent State University Press, 1994).
111. ZHANG, Shu Guang, *Mao's Military Romanticism: China and the Korean War, 1950–1953* (Lawrence: University Press of Kansas, 1995).
112. ZUBOK, Vladislav and PLESHAKOV, Constantine, *Inside the Kremlin's Cold War: From Stalin to Kruschev* (London: Harvard University Press, 1996).

Index

131

17304333R10087

Made in the USA
Middletown, DE
17 January 2015